Economics at Large

Economics at Large

An Advanced Textbook
on Macro-Economics

C. G. F. Simkin

University of Auckland

Weidenfeld and Nicolson
5 Winsley Street London W1

SBN 297 76327 X

Printed in Great Britain by
Morrison and Gibb Limited, London and Edinburgh

To my students

Contents

Preface   xi

PART 1   BASIC IDEAS

Chapter 1   **Social accounting**   3

1.1   The basic system
1.2   Activities and transactions
1.3   Dummies and imputations
1.4   Stocks, depreciation, banking and insurance
1.5   Government transactions
1.6   Capital account and external account
1.7   Symbols and identities

Chapter 2   **Macro-economic theory**   18

2.1   The possibility
2.2   Basic relations
2.3   The multiplier model
2.4   The multiplier-accelerator model
2.5   A lagged multiplier-accelerator model
2.6   Capital-output models
2.7   Which is best?
Appendix   Linear difference equations

Chapter 3   **A note on econometric tests**   40

PART 2   EMPIRICAL FUNCTIONS AND MODELS

Chapter 4   **Private consumption**   49

4.1   The propensity to consume
4.2   The relative and permanent income hypotheses

4.3 The influence of income distribution
4.4 The influence of interest or liquidity
4.5 Recent findings
4.6 Conclusions

Chapter 5 **Private investment**   59

5.1 The propensity to invest
5.2 The pure acceleration principle and the inventory cycle
5.3 The capacity principle and capital-output models
5.4 Recent findings

Chapter 6 **Liquidity**   69

6.1 Key notions
6.2 Empirical work
6.3 Conclusion

Chapter 7 **Foreign trade**   77

7.1 Imports
7.2 Exports

Chapter 8 **Labour**   82

8.1 Production functions and perfect competition
8.2 Empirical results

Chapter 9 **Some practical models**   88

9.1 A simple forecasting model for the United States
9.2 A Dutch planning model
9.3 A recent model for New Zealand

PART 3   INTERINDUSTRY ANALYSIS

Chapter 10 **Interindustry accounting**   99

10.1 Breaking down the production account
10.2 Problems of classification

10.3   Examples of transactions matrices
10.4   A suggested amalgamation

Chapter 11   **The input-output model and
                    applications**   110

11.1   The open Leontief model
11.2   Requirements for labour and imports
11.3   Effects of changes in final demand
11.4   Price analysis
11.5   Effects of changes in wage rates or import prices
11.6   The role of input-output analysis
11.7   Limitations of the analysis

PART 4   POLICY PROBLEMS

Chapter 12   **Can the economy regulate itself?**   125

12.1   The Ricardo-Wicksell model
12.2   Keynes's critique
12.3   Klein's scepticism
12.4   Patinkin and the real balance effect
12.5   Kaldor and profit changes
12.6   The need for policy

Chapter 13   **Fiscal policy**   145

13.1   Targets and instruments
13.2   Fiscal instruments
13.3   Functional finance
13.4   Built-in stabilizers
13.5   Fiscal policy and demand inflation

Chapter 14   **Monetary policy**   159

14.1   Monetary instruments
14.2   Money, interest and spending
14.3   Monetary policy and liquidity

Chapter 15 **Income policy** 168

15.1 Wages policy and full employment
15.2 Cost-push versus demand-pull inflation
15.3 Wages policy in the Netherlands
15.4 Other attempts

Chapter 16 **Foreign trade policy** 185

16.1 The alternatives
16.2 Import controls
16.3 Devaluation in a small country
16.4 Devaluation with much unemployment
16.5 Devaluation with little unemployment

Index 201

Preface

This book has been written to help the increasing number of students who are advancing in economics and who have had the good sense to acquire enough mathematics to follow occasional arguments involving algebra and calculus. It presupposes, accordingly, an understanding of elementary economics through study of such a book as Lipsey's *Positive Economics* or Samuelson's *Economics* and, if not a first-year university course in mathematics, a grasp of such a book as Allen's *Mathematical Analysis for Economists* or Lipsey and Archibald's *Introduction to the Mathematical Treatment of Economics*.

In this respect it is an advanced textbook, more concise than most others in the field, because it refrains from spelling out elementary points and uses mathematics wherever this is needed to make arguments precise or reasonably brief. But there are two more important reasons for a somewhat mathematical treatment, one pedagogical and the other utilitarian. The pedagogical reason is that the book seeks to bridge the considerable gap between the level of texts, written for a mass market, and that of journal articles or other primary works to which advanced students should be referred but with which they often, naturally, find difficulty. The utilitarian reason is that constant reference has been made here to empirical work in order to check and shape macro-analysis so as to guide its application to important problems of economic policy. Such testing is largely statistical, and many important applications involve quantitative models for forecasting or planning the behaviour of an economy.

The book covers a wide range but properly leaves much to teachers in elaborating points of special interest or difficulty, and in giving further references. No textbook can be anything like a perfect substitute for a good teacher, and this one will have achieved its purpose if teachers and students find it a useful aid or guide for studying the nature, scope and applications of macro-economic analysis.

Part I sets out the basic tools of macro-economics—social accounts and macro-models—and offers some guidance about interpreting econometric equations which test these models. Students should read most of Chapter 1 and the first three sections of Chapter 2 fairly carefully in order to consolidate their first-year work on macro-economics. The remainder of Chapter 2, however, and Chapter 3 can be read first rather quickly, and then referred to more carefully as various functions, models and empirical equations appear in Part II.

Interindustry analysis, also important for economic planning, is explained in Part III, where Chapter 10 requires reference back to Chapter 1, and Chapter 11 has affinities to Chapter 2. Part IV deals with policy problems and here a geometrical treatment suffices for the problems discussed in Chapter 12, and later chapters require little further mathematical argument until the discussion of devaluation in the final chapter.

I would express my thanks to Professor R. G. Lipsey for advice about this book, and to both the University of Essex and the Commonwealth Scholarships Commission for enabling me to complete it during my tenure of a Visiting Commonwealth Professorship in 1966–7. I am also grateful to Professor A. R. Bergstrom for helpful discussion about Chapters 3 and 9.3, and to Miss J. Irwin for invaluable secretarial assistance.

C. G. F. Simkin

Part One
Basic Ideas

CHAPTER 1

Social Accounting

1.1 The Basic System

No country, these days, can be respectable internationally unless its official statisticians publish a set of social accounts that show the national income and, more important, the ways in which this has been produced and used. Such figures give some kind of answer to a wide range of statistical questions; for example, how the country's income compares with those of other countries, how rapidly its production is growing, how heavily its citizens are taxed, how much is being saved, or how dependent the economy is upon foreign trade.

But social accounts do more than meet statistical curiosity. Their main function is to help governments nudge, guide or control economic conditions in an endeavour to discharge responsibilities they have now assumed for keeping employment at a high level, preventing undue inflation of prices, safeguarding resources of foreign exchange or promoting economic growth. The accounts are also increasingly used by larger businesses or trade associations for assessing their own performance and prospects in the light of quantitative information about the whole economy or its various sectors.

Although attempts at estimating national income go back to the seventeenth century, it was not until the 1939–1945 War that social accounts were first prepared. The pioneers were the United Kingdom and the United States, but other countries soon followed suit, helped by methodological advice from the United Nations Organization. The usefulness of social accounts, especially for international purposes, is obviously greatest if there is reasonable consistency and uniformity in the basic

3

statistical definitions and in the basic accounting framework. By 1966 the United Nations Organization was able to publish tables of the more important social accounting aggregates for 126 countries. Not all of them had closely followed its recommendations, but more than minor departures from uniformity are now uncommon in the social accounts of non-communist countries. (Accounts of communist countries differ mainly in a Marxian limitation of the concept of production to material goods and only those services which are directly associated with such goods.)

Prevailing consensus about basic conventions of social accounting is illustrated by Table 1.1, which displays a matrix for a hypothetical set of social accounts, reduced to bare essentials. There are five accounts covering the main sectors of economic activity; viz.

I   National Production and Income Account
II Private Income and Expenditure Account
III Government Income and Expenditure Account
IV National Capital Account
V   External Account

Receipts of one account from other accounts are shown along the rows of the matrix, and its payments to other accounts down the columns. The ancient art of double entry bookkeeping, used by social as well as by business accountants, requires simultaneous record of any transaction both as a receipt and as a payment. Here this requirement is simply met by the fact that any single entry in the matrix must be both in a particular row and in a particular column. And, because accounting definitions are always so framed as to make the two sides of any account balance, a row total for any section in the matrix equals the total for its corresponding column.

1.2 Activities and Transactions
This division of transactions between five summary accounts reflects a view about both the main types of economic activity and the main types of transactions. Account I summarizes all

4

Table 1.1 Illustrative Matrix of Social Accounts

Payments to	Transaction	I	II	III	IV	V	Totals
I	Sales of goods and services	—	800 (C)	190 (G)	250	260a (X)	1,500
	Less imports	—	—	—	—	−245a (M)	1,255 (GNP)
	Less depreciation	—	—	—	−125	—	1,130 (Y_m)
	Less net transfers	—	—	−130 (T_i)	—	—	1,000 (Y_f)
II	Factor incomes	990 (Y_p)	—	—	—	—	—
	Less net transfers	—	—	−90 (T_d)	—	—	900 (Y_d)
III	Factor incomes	10 (Y_g)	—	—	—	—	—
	Less net foreign transfers	—	—	—	—	−5 (T_f)	5
IV	Saving	—	100 (S_p)	35 (S_g)	—	−10 (S_f)	125 (S)
Totals		1,000 (Y)	900	5	125 (I)	0	—

a Includes net property income.

activities that can be described as *production*, and includes all transactions by *businesses*, whether these are private or public enterprises. *Consumption*, which has long been regarded as the ultimate purpose of production, is split between the two income accounts for the private and government sectors. The reason for the split is that private consumers are concerned with satisfying their own or their households' wants, whereas the non-business activities of government are concerned with the satisfaction of collective wants for defence, police, justice, public health, and so on. Not all production, however, goes to meet requirements for consumption within the current accounting period. Some goes to provide for future consumption by adding to stocks of goods or to stocks of equipment and

5

buildings. This part is called *capital formation*, an activity which is reflected in the National Capital Account.

There remains the account for the *external sector*. It is needed to complete the application of double entry bookkeeping to a summary record of the economy's transactions, and is purely formal in the sense that other countries are included only to the extent that they have transactions with the recording country. But it has just as much significance as any other social account, at least for a country which is markedly dependent on external transactions, because it provides information about the current balance of payments.

It will be noticed that, within the accounts, transactions are classified as sales of goods or services, factor incomes and net transfers. *Sales* in the production account do not show transactions connected with goods or services that are both produced and used as inputs for producing other goods or services during the accounting period. These are called *intermediate* goods or services and do not appear here because, on aggregation over the whole economy, receipts from their sale must cancel out against payments for their current use. (That is why the matrix has a zero diagonal.) Intermediate outputs obviously include raw or semi-finished materials; e.g. coal which is mined and used, within the accounting period, to generate electricity. But some materials can appear as *final outputs*, and must do so if their current production exceeds their current use. The excess, that is, goes either to increase stocks of materials, and hence appears as a sale to the national capital account, or else goes to exports and appears as a sale to the external sector. Imports of materials, likewise, appear as purchases of the production account from the external sector.

The main payments from the production account are for current services of labour, management and such property as is used in production. These services are the factors of production, and the corresponding payments of salaries or wages, profits and interest, dividends or rents are called *factor incomes*. They contrast with *transfers*, or income receipts that do not correspond to the rendering of any current productive service; e.g. pensions, scholarships, monetary social security benefits paid to the private sector, or taxes paid to the government sector. Net transfer receipts in the production account are subsidies less indirect taxes, and those in the private income account are pensions, scholarships, or other monetary benefits less direct taxes. Both net transfers are large negative items because government has to spend most tax receipts in providing for collective wants.

1.3 Dummies and Imputations

Sales and factor payments include some matching transactions that are of a dummy or imputed nature. Consider the first receipt (800) of the production account, which is also the payment of the private sector for its own consumption (C). This includes all actual sales of enterprises to persons or households, other than those of a capital type which, of course, are posted to the national capital account. It also includes, however, factor payments by households or other non-profit making institutions in the private sector; e.g. wages paid to servants in private homes or to staff employed by religious, charitable and recreational associations. If the test of production is provision for wants, and a test of wants payment for means of satisfying them, then the work of a servant in a household is just as much a contribution to production as that of those who supply the whisky it drinks; and the work of a greenkeeper in a golf-club is just as productive as that of those who supply the gear its members use. Similar considerations apply to the second receipt (190) which represents the consumption expenditure (G) of pure government. This item includes not only purchases of goods by non-business departments but also factor incomes which they pay in order to meet collective wants; people in these departments are doing work which is just as productive as that of firms which supply the departments with typewriters or electricity. Production is thus a wider concept than business activities. But to include other activities in the national production account we have, besides posting factor incomes paid by non-business units to the payments side of the account, to treat the value of their work as a *dummy sale* to private or government income account.

Nor are these the only dummy sales. The fifth receipt (260) for exports (X) includes receipts from factor services supplied to foreigners. Some of these services are not directly supplied by business but come from property owned in other countries by private individuals and perhaps also by government. Such property income is included in the production account as a dummy sale, just as property income received from abroad is treated as a corresponding payment, by that account, of factor income. Imports, too, include property income paid to residents of other countries, and some of this is paid by government or by non-business units in the private sector.

Dummy sales may look odd but have straightforward explanations. *Imputations* are more difficult, and hence are applied in a less wholehearted way. The basic idea behind them is that some production involves no monetary transactions but, if it is to be properly included in the national production account, has to have a monetary value assigned to it.

In the private sector there is an obvious need for imputation in regard to factor incomes which are partly received in kind. The produce consumed by farmers who have raised it is profit-in-kind, and the food or accommodation supplied to farm workers is wages-in-kind, as is the food and accommodation supplied to nurses, sailors or hotel workers and the free meals in workers' canteens. There are difficulties in valuing such incomes-in-kind but the problem has to be tackled, not only by social accountants but also by tax-gatherers and wage-negotiators. For similar reasons net rents are imputed as part of the factor income of those who occupy their own houses; for if an owner moved out he could increase his money income by renting the house to someone else, and the services of houses are just as much a part of production as are outputs of housing materials.

Why not go further by including imputed rentals for other types of consumer assets which could also be rented commercially: TV sets, motor-cars, refrigerators, furniture, etc? In principle, such rentals ought to be included but most statisticians shrink from the difficulty of measuring them. They also shrink from estimating the value of work performed by people in, and for, their own households. But why limit productive labour to paid labour? Does production really fall if a man marries his housekeeper or if, on retirement, he sacks his gardener and takes over the same work himself? Clearly not; yet there are great difficulties in knowing, let alone valuing, all the work households do in cooking their food, maintaining their homes, growing their vegetables, repairing their cars, and so on. In some cases, moreover, there would be difficulties about drawing a line between productive and recreational activity.

The United Nations Organization sanctions this neglect by giving rules which, as it says, 'result in omitting from production the net amount of all non-primary production performed by producers outside their own trades and consumed by themselves'. This looks odd for a world organization concerned with underdeveloped countries; for in these countries, largely dependent upon subsistence farming, peasant families provide much for themselves that families in advanced countries buy. Women make clothing, preserve foods, gather fuel and fetch water; men, often with the unpaid help of friends, build their own simple houses, furniture and boats. The United Nations' rules, accordingly, must lead to estimates which overstate the poverty of underdeveloped countries, and so understate their economic achievements.

1.4 Stocks, Depreciation, Banking and Insurance

Businessmen were aware of problems of imputation in regard to capital formation long before social accounting began. Additions to stocks of goods, finished or unfinished, were recognized as a profit-in-kind, and depreciation of fixed assets through use or obsolescence as a loss-in-kind. But there are problems about imputing values to changes in stocks or to depreciation of fixed assets, and differences about their solution.

Being concerned to measure real productive flows as far as possible, social accountants try to measure the current value of net additions to stock. Business accountants, however, use methods which may give different answers. The differences can be simply expressed by using a few symbols:

q = quantity of stocks at the beginning of the current accounting period

$q + \Delta q$ = quantity of stocks at the end of the period

p = average price over the previous period

$p + \Delta p$ = average price over the current period

a = current additions to quantity of stocks

u = current usages from stock

The social accounting valuation of current net additions to stock is always:

$$[p + \Delta p] \, \Delta q.$$

This compares with:

(a) $[a - u] [p + \Delta p] = [p + \Delta p] \, \Delta q$ if $\Delta q > o$

(b) $[u - a]p = p\Delta q$ if $\Delta q < o$

for the LIFO method (last-in, first-out); and with

(a) $a[p + \Delta p] - up = p\Delta q + a\Delta p$ if $q > u$

(b) $[a - u] [p + \Delta p] + q\Delta p = [p + \Delta p] \, \Delta q + q\Delta p$ if $q < u$

for the FIFO method (first-in, first-out).

It is less easy to give a similar statement for the other common business method of valuing opening stock at the lower of cost or previous market price, and final stock at the lower of cost or current market price. But if average prices over the year apply in both cases, current net additions to stock could be expressed as

(a) $p[q + \Delta q] - pq = p\Delta q$ if $\Delta p > o$

(b) $[p + \Delta p] [q + \Delta q] - [p + \Delta p]q = [p + \Delta p]\Delta q$ if $\Delta p < o$

FIFO, clearly, gives larger estimates of net additions to stock than the social accounting method. The other two business methods give much closer results, as LIFO coincides with the social accounting method if stocks increase, and the method of using the lower of cost or market price coincides with it if prices fall.

Depreciation, or allowance for capital consumption of fixed assets, presents greater difficulties. Businesses, and also tax authorities, usually reckon depreciation at original cost, a procedure which is clearly unsatisfactory if prices change much over the working life of assets. Social accountants, therefore, usually prefer a basis of replacement cost. The most ambitious attempt to apply this basis has been in the United Kingdom, where estimates have been made of the current value of various types of assets by applying the prices of new, but similar, assets to the old. These estimates are then divided by other estimates, or assumptions, about working lives so as to reach proper depreciation allowances for each type of asset. But a basic difficulty still remains; capital assets, in a world of quite rapid technological change, are seldom replaced by anything like identical assets. Some authorities, impressed by the difficulty, prefer to value production gross of depreciation, a procedure, of course, that merely evades the problem.

Capital formation, whether reckoned gross or net of depreciation, includes more than additions made by businesses to their stocks of goods, equipment or buildings. It also includes additions to houses made by the private sector or, in these days of public housing, by government. The inclusion is consistent with the treatment of net owner-rentals as an imputed factor income, and also with the somewhat arbitrary exclusion of other consumer durables from a similar treatment.

Government further undertakes much investment in non-commercial assets, if only to help provision of the collective wants which it has to meet. New roads, bridges, lighthouses, police stations, hospitals, museums, departmental buildings, schools and research stations are a few examples of this sort of investment. It is practicable to estimate depreciation for buildings and some equipment, but not even the United Kingdom attempts to estimate depreciation of roads; their upkeep is charged to current expenditure.

Another problem of imputation arises in connection with financial intermediaries, especially banks and life insurance offices, which borrow money from depositors or, in effect, from

11

policyholders at a lower rate than is charged for loans. If, as with other business concerns, their net contributions to national production were taken as equal to apparent net payments of factor incomes – salaries, wages, profits and net interest – there would be a large negative item for net interest paid, so that their contributions to production might well appear to be negative. In order to avoid such absurd understatement, the United Nations Organization recommends the imputation of an extra interest payment to depositors or policyholders sufficient to make the net interest payments zero. The contribution of financial intermediaries to production would then match their payments of salaries, wages and profits. There has, of course, to be added to the other side of the production account an equal imputed charge to depositors and policyholders so that the account balances. Such imputation is justified by the consideration that clients receive many services either free or well below cost; e.g. cheque facilities or management of policyholders' accumulated funds. These services are an interest-in-kind, and have to be given an imputed value if a complete estimate of national production is to be reached.

The United States and many other countries follow this recommended procedure. But the United Kingdom dodges it because of difficulties in assuming that all free or subsidized banking services accrue to depositors, as distinct from borrowers, and in allocating such a cost between the private and other sectors. Imputations for these services to domestic businesses would net out in the production account as an intermediate service, so that countries making this imputation assign it wholly, but not quite accurately, to the private sector; in principle, some of the imputation should be assigned to government or to the external sector.

1.5 Government Transactions

We have, in discussing the production account, also covered most items of the interlocking income and expenditure accounts. It has been shown that factor incomes comprise both actual and imputed payments for work and for current use of property in domestic production plus net property income received from foreign assets. Wages include those received in kind, as well as in cash, and must also include hidden wages such as employers' payments to social security funds, pension schemes or insurance schemes which benefit their workers. (Employees' compensation, however, is net of any allowable expenses of earning a particular livelihood.) Property income includes imputed owner-rentals from houses, and imputed interest to depositors or policyholders.

Although any property income received from abroad is counted as factor income, and any payment abroad of property income as a deduction from national production, this does not always hold for the domestic scene. The exception here is that interest paid by government to *residents* on non-commercial public debt is treated as a transfer payment or income. We have, then, the apparently odd position that interest received by a resident from a foreign government is factor income, but interest received from his own government is transfer income.

It is not hard to justify the procedure so far as foreign interest receipts or payments are concerned. They have, ultimately at least, to be paid for by a surplus of exports over imports, and so correspond to productive efforts in achieving the necessary trading surplus. Nor is it hard to justify the treatment of internal interest payments on *unproductive* public debt, e.g. war debt, as a transfer of income from taxpayers to bondholders. But some public debt is productive. Interest, of course, on debt which has financed public enterprises is included in the production account and, along with other interest payments from that account, is treated as factor income. The problem relates to non-commercial debt owed by the pure government sector.

In principle, interest paid to residents on productive, non-commercial debt, such as that raised for transportation, health or educational facilities should be counted as factor income if the corresponding activities are, as is usual, regarded as part of national production. Yet this is rarely attempted, even in countries where comparatively little government debt represents war debt. One reason, perhaps, is the practical difficulty of separating productive government debt from other borrowings used to finance overall budgetary deficits, in the main, wartime deficits; for this would require a valuation of the whole stock of non-commercial assests – a formidable problem.

(*Capital gains* are also treated as a transfer – from the buyer of an asset to the seller. It is not uncommon for land values, in a growing community, to rise sharply in value, or for physical assets to do this during a period of inflation. There is no gain to national production associated with sales of such assets, although, like other transfers, capital gains increase the individual incomes of recipients.)

A minor point is the treatment of profits from public enterprises. These are usually included as a payment of factor income from the production account to the government account. But many public enterprises, such as the Post Office, may fix prices at levels well above cost in order to increase public revenue, or some government enterprises, e.g. state housing, may set prices well below cost in order to help a particular group of consumers. The United Nations Organization recommends that, where the monopoly position of a public enterprise is deliberately used to yield a substantial profit, the surplus profit should be treated as an indirect tax, i.e. as a *transfer* from the production account. Where, similarly, losses are deliberate, they should be treated as subsidies.

1.6 Capital Account and External Account

Savings may be defined as the excess of an income and expenditure account, and are credited to national capital account. The definition, however, applies only to savings net of depreciation, which is itself a credit to national capital account from the production account. If, as might well be desirable, there were separate capital accounts for each sector, they would have to include another item for net borrowing or lending between sectors. But, in a closed economy, such net loans would cancel out on aggregation into a national capital account or, in an open economy, would include only net loans made to, or received from, the external sector.

Our matrix shows a uniform treatment along the row of the

national capital account by listing net private, government and foreign saving, the total of which is net domestic capital formation or investment. The item for net foreign saving is negative in our example, meaning that some part of domestic saving has gone into acquiring foreign assets as well as into financing domestic capital formation.

No row appears in the matrix for the external sector, merely because of the very summary nature of the example, which emphasizes essentials and symmetry. It is quite easy to prepare a two-sided external account from column V, which has summed to zero. The negative items in this column are receipts of the external sector, and the positive items its balancing payments. These receipts come from the sale of goods or services imported plus property income paid abroad, (including interest on the government debt held by foreigners), plus foreign transfers from government account and representing such items as grants made to developing countries. Payments relate to exports and the net property income received from abroad by residents of the country whose accounts we are considering. There is a deficit in our hypothetical external account, representing capital receipts accruing to other countries from sale of financial assets; e.g. holdings of gold or foreign currencies, bonds of foreign governments, shares in foreign companies, loans to foreigners, and businesses, productive assets or houses owned in foreign countries.

1.7 Symbols and Identities
The preceding discussion should have brought out the remarkable achievement of social accounting in summarizing a country's economic transactions and in giving a broad picture of their structure. It should also have tempered enthusiasm for this achievement by some appreciation of the arbitrary elements in social accounting arising from difficulties of imputation and other problems. Even the best set of social accounts is far from having any claim to absolute precision and there are, inevitably, considerable differences between the best and the worst.

Problems of measurement, and improving measurement, of

the vast mass of economic transactions will not be further considered here. Our immediate aim is simply to exhibit a number of important accounting relations that provide the basis of a relatively new branch of economic analysis known as macro-economics. These relations, fortunately, are few and, problems of measurement aside, fairly straightforward.

They are expressed by symbols, which are convenient for shorthand expression and necessary for the models which will be used to explain movements in national income or its components. First are symbols for various types of income:

Y_m = net national income or product at market prices
Y_f = net national income or product at factor cost
Y_d = disposable private income.

These are related to net transfers:

T_i = indirect taxes less subsidies
$Y_g + T_d$ = government factor income plus direct taxes less income transfers from government.

We have, using these symbols and figures in the matrix,

(1) $Y_f = Y_m - T_i$ or $1,000 = 1,130 - 130$
(2) $Y_d = Y_f - Y_g - T_d$ or $900 = 1,000 - 10 - 90$.

Net national expenditures are associated with these symbols:

C = private consumption
G = government consumption
I = net domestic capital formation or investment
X = exports of goods and services plus property income received from the external sector
M = imports of goods and services plus property income paid to the external sector
S = net saving, private (S_p) government (S_g) and foreign (S_f).

We now have

(3) $Y_m = C + I + G + X - M$ or $1,130 = 800 + 125 + 190 + 260 - 245$

16

Further

(4) $\quad S = S_p + S_g + S_f$ or $125 = 100 + 35 - 10$
$$= (Y_d - C) + (T_i + T_d - T_f - G) + (M + T_f - X)$$
i.e.

(5) $\quad S = Y_m - (C + G + X - M) = I.$

This last result is the famous statistical identity, following from social accounting definitions, that aggregate saving equals aggregate investment.

References

For a simple comprehensive view of the social accounting scheme see:
R. Stone and G. Croft-Murray, *Social Accounting and Economic Models*, Chs. I and II,
and for a more extended account:
H. C. Edey and A. T. Peacock, *National Income and Social Accounting*, Part I,
W. Beckerman, *An Introduction to National Income Analysis*, London, 1968.
For authoritative, more technical references, see:
United Nations, *Measurement of National Income and Construction of Social Accounts*, Geneva, 1957.
Central Statistical Office, *National Income Statistics*, H.M.S.O., 1956.
U.S. Department of Commerce, *National Income*, 1954 Edition.
A good general discussion, from the standpoint of basic principles, is given by:
R. Stone, 'Functions and Criteria of a System of Social Accounting', *Income and Wealth*, Series I, 1951.
and more ambitious discussions by:
Ingvar Ohlssen, *On National Accounting*. Stockholm, 1953.
M. Yanovsky, *Anatomy of Social Accounting Systems*, London, 1965.

CHAPTER 2

Macro-economic Theory

2.1 The Possibility

Social accounting has undoubtedly proved useful in giving comprehensive summaries of transactions between the various sectors of an economy, and so of its activities. But no accounts, by themselves, can tell us more than what has happened. If social accounts are to be used for explaining what has happened, for predicting what is likely to happen or for influencing what should happen, then they must be associated with a theory about the behaviour of macro-economic variables such as those recorded in the social accounts.

How can we reach such a theory? Most transactions arise from the behaviour of consumers or businessmen in particular markets, and there is a well-developed micro-economic theory which explains their behaviour in these markets. Expenditures, for example, on a particular j-th commodity would be formally explained by an equation of the type,

$$e_j = f_j (y_1, y_2, ..., y_m; p_1, p_2, ..., p_n, a_1, a_2, ..., a_q)$$

where e_j denotes total expenditure on this j-th commodity and f_j is a functional relation which makes its value depend upon the incomes of the m individual buyers (the y's), the prices of all n commodities in the economy (the p's), and upon q autonomous or non-economic influences (the a's), such as the weather or a change in fashion. It would seem that we ought to derive macro-economic theory by aggregating such micro-economic equations.

We can, however, aggregate them only if they have a linear form

$$e_j = a_{j1}y_1 + a_{j2}y_2 + ... + a_{jm}y_m + \beta_{j1}p_1 + \beta_{j2}p_2 + ... + \beta_{jn}p_n + \gamma_{j1}a_1$$
$$+ \gamma_{j2}a_2 + ... + \gamma_{jq}a_q$$

18

or if they can be reduced to a linear form. Exponential relations, for example

$$e_j = y_1^{a_{j1}} y_2^{a_{j2}} \ldots y_m^{a_{jm}} p_1^{\beta_{j1}} p_2^{\beta_{j2}} \ldots p_n^{\beta_{jn}} a_1^{\gamma_{j1}} a_2^{\gamma_{j2}} \ldots a_q^{\gamma_{jq}}$$

become linear when logarithmic values are taken; for then

$$\begin{aligned} \text{Log } e_j = a_{j1} \text{ Log } y_1 + a_{j2} \text{ Log } y_2 + \ldots + a_{jm} \text{ Log } y_m + \beta_{j1} \text{ Log } p_1 \\ + \beta_{j2} \text{ Log } p_2 + \ldots + \beta_{jn} \text{ Log } p_n + \gamma_{j1} \text{ Log } a_1 + \gamma_{j2} \text{ Log } a_2 \\ + \ldots + \gamma_{jq} \text{ Log } a_q \end{aligned}$$

the exponential form has the advantage that the a's can be interpreted as income elasticities of demand and the β's as price elasticities).

Aggregation would then lead to

$$\begin{aligned} E = \sum_{j=1}^{n} e_j = (\Sigma_j a_{j1}) y_1 + \ldots + (\Sigma_j a_{jm}) y_m + (\Sigma_j \beta_{j1}) p_1 + \ldots + (\Sigma_j \beta_{jn}) p_n \\ + (\Sigma_j \gamma_{j1}) a_1 + \ldots + (\Sigma_j \gamma_{jq}) a_q \end{aligned}$$

or, using the symbols for double summation over all incomes and all commodities,

$$E = \sum_j e_j = \sum_i \sum_j a_{ji} y_i + \sum_k \sum_j \beta_{jk} p_k + \sum_l \sum_j \gamma_{lj}, a_l$$

$$i = 1, \ldots, m$$
$$j, k = 1, \ldots, n$$
$$l = 1, \ldots, q.$$

This is the first step towards a macro-economic relation. But it has a basic difficulty. No micro-economic function, still less all, need have a linear form or be reducible to such a form. A macro-economic relation can thus be satisfactory only to the extent that linear forms are good approximations to underlying micro-economic relations. Here is one inevitable looseness of macro-economics.

There are others, too. In macro-economics we have to work, not with the whole range of individual incomes and particular prices, but with a few aggregates of incomes or averages of prices. Suppose we use a single aggregate of incomes, Y, a single index of prices, P, and a single average of autonomous influences, A, so that our macro-economic relation is

$$E = AY + BP + \Gamma A.$$

It may now be seen (by substitution) that this relation is fully consistent with our first step from micro-economic relations only if we have the peculiar weighted averages,

$$A = \frac{1}{m} \sum_i \sum_j a_{ji}, \quad Y = \frac{m \sum_i \sum_j a_{ji} y_i}{\sum_i \sum_j a_{ji}},$$

$$B = \sum_k \sum_j \beta_{jk}, \quad P = \frac{\sum_k \sum_j \beta_{jk} p_k}{\sum_k \sum_j \beta_{jk}},$$

$$\Gamma = \sum_l \sum_j \gamma_{jl}, \quad A = \frac{\sum_l \sum_j \gamma_{jl} a_l}{\sum_l \sum_j \gamma_{jl}}.$$

Now it is obvious that the above expression for aggregate income differs from the simple sum which appears in the social accounts, i.e. from

$$Y = \sum_i y_i.$$

It involves an impossible weighting of individual incomes according to each consumer's propensity to spend from his income on all commodities; (for we could put $\sum_i (\sum_j a_{ji}) y_i = \sum_i A_i y_i$). No country could ascertain such weights, yet macro-economics depends upon the extent to which a simple aggregate of incomes is a good approximation to this theoretical aggregate.

The above price index, similarly, differs from any ordinary price index in its impossible requirement of weighting particular prices by double sums of price coefficients from the individual demand functions; (if these were linear in logarithmic values the weights would involve direct- and cross-price elasticities of demand). This difficulty is less serious than that for income. In micro-economics relative prices are important because they cause shifts in demands or supplies between particular markets, but these shifts tend to cancel out on aggregation. Macro-economics, accordingly, neglects prices or else represents them by only a few indices for sectors which are obviously affected by broad changes in relative prices; e.g. domestic and export prices whose relation affects exports or imports.

Autonomous influences in particular markets also tend to cancel out on aggregation. Some, however, have a strong residual influence on the whole economy; e.g. a monsoon failure in India or a large defence cut in the United Kingdom. Even if macro-economics has fewer autonomous influences to reckon with, this does not point to a basic difference from micro-economics. By definition, such influences are unexplained by economic analysis of either variety.

The real difference is that, although macro-economic relations are suggested by micro-economic theory, they cannot be rigorously derived from it because of the need for drastic simplifications in regard to form of functions and measurement of variables. The simplifications have to be made in order to reach a manageable theory about the behaviour of the economy or its main sectors, but they cannot be trusted until they have proved useful for this purpose. Macro-economics does not differ from any type of scientific theory in having to submit to the ultimate test of surviving empirical refutation. It does, however, differ from micro-economics in having a looser structure and, because of somewhat arbitrary choice between alternative classifications of sectors, degree of aggregation of variables or inclusion of variables, a more *ad hoc* character. For these reasons, it is important to keep macro-economic analysis as much as possible in touch with empirical work, as later chapters will emphasize.

2.2 Basic Relations

With such preliminary explanation and warning about the character of macro-economic theory, we proceed to consider its general structure. This is best revealed by the 'models' which play so large a role in formulating and testing the theory.

A model may be described as a set of equations which are together just sufficient for explaining the set of variables under investigation. A macro-economic model has various types of equations – identities, technical relations and behaviour relations. *Identities* include definitional relations from the social accounts, such as those exhibited in 1.7. There we saw that national expenditure at market prices could be broken down into

$$Y_m = C + G + I + X - M,$$

that national income was national expenditure at factor cost or

$$Y_f = Y_m - T_i$$

and that private disposable income was national income less net direct taxes and government trading profits,

$$Y_d = Y_f - (T_d + Y_g).$$

If we can ignore government trading profits and make the simplifying assumption that net taxes are proportional to national income, i.e. if

$$T_i = t_i Y_f$$
$$T_d = t_d Y_f$$

then we can derive a particular *technical relation* between disposable private income and national expenditure at market prices. For we have

$$Y_d = Y_f - t_d Y_f = (1 - t_d)\ Y_f$$
$$Y_f = Y_m - t_i\ Y_f = \left(\frac{1}{1 + t_i}\right) Y_m$$

and hence

$$Y_d = \left(\frac{1 - t_d}{1 + t_i}\right) Y_m.$$

Another example of a technical relation would be a production function which related national output to aggregate factor inputs, or a minimum practical ratio between stocks and steady turnover.

Macro-economics uses identities and technical relations for models, but its fundamental idea is that one or more of the components of national expenditure depends, in a strong way, upon national income itself. The dependent components can be denoted by E and the other autonomous components by A, so that we write

$$Y_m = E + A.$$

The dependence of E upon income is expressed by a *behaviour relation* such as the previous section described. The simplest, if not the most plausible, behaviour relation for E is that it is proportional to disposable private income; i.e.

$$E = e Y_d.$$

Making use of our technical relation we can thus express the behaviour relation as

$$E = e \left(\frac{1 - t_d}{1 + t_i} \right) Y_m = \epsilon Y_m.$$

From now on we can drop the subscript m, and take Y as representing net national expenditure or, what is the same thing, as national income at market prices.

2.3 The Multiplier Model
The preceding relations constitute the *unlagged multiplier* model which has been made familiar by elementary textbooks; viz.

$$Y = E + A$$
$$E = \epsilon Y$$

where ϵ may be called the tax-adjusted marginal propensity to spend. From these two equations we readily obtain the result

$$Y = \left(\frac{1}{1 - \epsilon} \right) A.$$

The expression in brackets is the 'multiplier', or the amount by which any change of autonomous expenditure has to be multiplied in order to find the corresponding change of income.

We need not suppose that dependent expenditure, E, is adjusted to income immediately. If, instead, we recognize a lag in the adjustment of spending to changes of income, and use a time subscript, θ, we obtain a *lagged multiplier* model; i.e.

$$Y_\theta = E_\theta + A$$
$$E_\theta = \epsilon Y_{\theta-1}$$

supposing that E lags behind Y by one period of time, a month, a quarter, or a year, depending upon the unit of time in which θ is measured.

Define now

$$y_\theta = Y_\theta - \left(\frac{1}{1-\epsilon}\right) A$$

and obtain from the income identity and the lagged spending function,

$$y_\theta = \epsilon Y_{\theta-1} + A - \left(\frac{1}{1-\epsilon}\right) A$$

$$= \epsilon \left[Y_{\theta-1} - \left(\frac{1}{1-\epsilon}\right) A \right]$$

$$= \epsilon y_{\theta-1} = \epsilon^2 y_{\theta-2} = \epsilon^3 y_{\theta-3} = \dots$$

i.e. $\qquad\qquad y_\theta = \epsilon^\theta y_0.$

Obviously, then

$$Y_\theta = \left(\frac{1}{1-\epsilon}\right) A + \epsilon^\theta y_0$$

and if, as must be supposed for a stable economy,

$\epsilon < 1$, then

$$\operatorname*{Lim}_{\theta \to \infty} Y_\theta = \left(\frac{1}{1-\epsilon}\right) A.$$

This means that a discontinuous increase of A leads eventually to a level of income which, as in the unlagged model, is $\left(\dfrac{1}{1-\epsilon}\right)$

24

times the new value of A. But, during the period when A changes, Y rises by exactly the increase of A, denoted by ΔA or y_0, because A is a component of Y and the other component, E, does not immediately rise owing to the lag. In the first period after the change, however, E rises by ϵy_0, a smaller amount than y_0 as $\epsilon < 1$, and Y rises further by just this amount. In the second period both E and Y rise by $\epsilon(\epsilon y_0)$ or $\epsilon^2 y_0$, a still smaller amount, and in the third period by $\epsilon(\epsilon^2 y_0) = \epsilon^3 y_0$. And so the process goes on, with Y rising by diminishing amounts until it reaches a new stable level, $\left(\dfrac{1}{1-\epsilon}\right)(A + \Delta A)$.

The process can be shown diagrammatically.

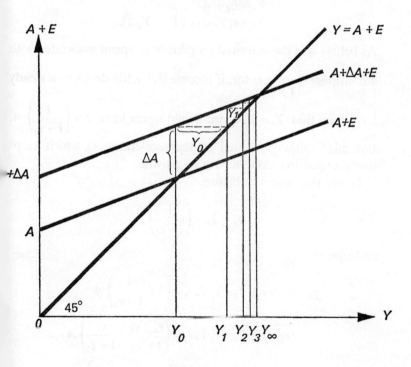

Figure 2.1

25

From an initial position where income was stable at OY_0, A rises to $A + \Delta A$ and income by $Y_1Y_0 = y_0 = \Delta A$ to OY_1. It then rises by $\epsilon(Y_0Y_1) = \epsilon y_0$ to OY_2, and next by $\epsilon(Y_1Y_2) = \epsilon^2 y_0$ to OY_3. The process stops when income reaches, by such diminishing steps, a new position of stability, OY_∞.

2.4 The Multiplier-Accelerator Model.

Income, at least in advanced countries, does not tend towards a steady *level* but rather undergoes more or less steady *growth*. Such growth may be explained by a multiplier-accelerator model in which E depends, not only on the *level* of income, but also upon the *change* of income. There are again two versions, one unlagged and the other lagged.

The unlagged version is

$$Y_\theta = E_\theta + A$$
$$E_\theta = \epsilon_1 Y_\theta + \epsilon_2 (Y_\theta - Y_{\theta-1}).$$

As before ϵ_1 is the marginal propensity to spend associated with a multiplier, $\left(\dfrac{1}{1-\epsilon_1}\right)$; for, if income did settle down to a steady level such that $Y_\theta = Y_{\theta-1}$, we would again have $Y = \left(\dfrac{1}{1-\epsilon_1}\right) A$. But this is now prevented by the accelerator, ϵ_2, which keeps income speeding along a path of growth.

To see this define as before,

$$y_\theta = Y_\theta - \left(\frac{1}{1-\epsilon_1}\right) A$$

and obtain

$$y_\theta = (\epsilon_1 + \epsilon_2)\, Y_\theta - \epsilon_2 Y_{\theta-1} + \left(1 - \frac{1}{1-\epsilon_1}\right) A$$

$$= (\epsilon_1 + \epsilon_2)\, Y_\theta - \epsilon_2 Y_{\theta-1} - \left(\frac{\epsilon_1 + \epsilon_2}{1-\epsilon_1} - \frac{\epsilon_2}{1-\epsilon_1}\right) A$$

$$= (\epsilon_1 + \epsilon_2)\, y_\theta - \epsilon_2 y_{\theta-1}$$

i.e. $$y_\theta = \left(\frac{\epsilon_2}{\epsilon_1 + \epsilon_2 - 1}\right) y_{\theta-1} = \left(\frac{\epsilon_2}{\epsilon_1 + \epsilon_2 - 1}\right)^2 y_{\theta-2} = \dots$$

$$= \left(\frac{\epsilon_2}{\epsilon_1 + \epsilon_2 - 1}\right)^\theta y_0.$$

Because $\epsilon_1 < 1$ we must have

$$\frac{\epsilon_2}{\epsilon_1 + \epsilon_2 - 1} > 1$$

so that once income reaches the level, $\left(\frac{1}{1-\epsilon_1}\right) A$, it now keeps rising. The growth of income above this level is

$$\frac{y_\theta - y_{\theta-1}}{y_{\theta-1}} = \frac{y_\theta}{y_{\theta-1}} - 1 = \frac{\epsilon_2}{\epsilon_1 + \epsilon_2 - 1} - 1$$

i.e. $$\frac{y_\theta - y_{\theta-1}}{y_{\theta-1}} = \frac{1 - \epsilon_1}{\epsilon_2 - (1 - \epsilon_1)}.$$

The well-known Harrod-Domar growth model is an important example of this unlagged multiplier-accelerator model. It ignores A but splits E into consumption and investment;

$$Y_\theta = E_\theta = C_\theta + I_\theta.$$

Consumption is adjusted to the current level of income

$$C_\theta = c Y_\theta$$

and hence saving is

$$S_\theta = Y_\theta - C_\theta = (1 - c) Y_\theta = s Y_\theta$$

where c is the marginal propensity to consume and s the marginal propensity to save. Investment, on the other hand, is adjusted to the current change of income,

$$I_\theta = a(Y_\theta - Y_{\theta-1}).$$

The reason is that capital is supposed for technical reasons, to be proportional to output and, as investment is the current increase of capital, investment will be proportional to the current increase of output. When saving is in balance with investment we have

$$S_\theta = s Y_\theta = a(Y_\theta - Y_{\theta-1}) = I_\theta$$

and hence

$$Y_\theta = \left(\frac{a}{a-s}\right) Y_{\theta-1}.$$

It follows that the growth rate of income is

$$\frac{Y_\theta - Y_{\theta-1}}{Y_{\theta-1}} = \left(\frac{a}{a-s}\right) - 1 = \frac{s}{a-s}$$

and, as

$$\frac{s}{a-s} = \frac{1-c}{a-(1-c)},$$

c corresponds to ϵ_1 and a to ϵ_2 in our general formula.

2.5 A Lagged Multiplier-Accelerator Model

A surprising change occurs if we introduce lags into the multiplier-accelerator model. Suppose that there is a uniform lag in adjusting expenditure both to level of income and to change of income so that the model becomes,

$$Y_\theta = E_\theta + A$$
$$E_\theta = \epsilon_1 Y_{\theta-1} + \epsilon_2 (Y_{\theta-1} - Y_{\theta-2}).$$

Then if, as before, we define

$$y_\theta = Y_\theta - \left(\frac{1}{1-\epsilon_1}\right) A$$

this now becomes

$$y_\theta = (\epsilon_1 + \epsilon_2) y_{\theta-1} - \epsilon_2 y_{\theta-2}.$$

There is no obvious solution to this equation – called a second order linear difference equation – but the Appendix shows that we can put

$$y_\theta = Pp^\theta + Qq^\theta$$

where

$$y_0 = P + Q$$
$$2p = (\epsilon_1 + \epsilon_2) + \sqrt{(\epsilon_1 + \epsilon_2)^2 - 4\epsilon_2}$$
$$2q = (\epsilon_1 + \epsilon_2) - \sqrt{(\epsilon_1 + \epsilon_2)^2 - 4\epsilon_2}$$
$$pq = \epsilon_2.$$

28

Four different types of change are then possible in income and also in its components.

The first two possibilities occur if

$$(\epsilon_1 + \epsilon_2)^2 > 4\epsilon_2$$

so that we are dealing with the square root of a positive number; p and q are then said to be real numbers.

(i) If p, the larger root, is less than unity then so is q, the smaller root, and both Pp^θ and Qq^θ must decrease as time goes on.

As, moreover,

$$Y_\theta = \left(\frac{1}{1+\epsilon_1}\right) A + Pp^\theta + Qq^\theta$$

it follows that

$$\operatorname*{Lim}_{\theta \to \infty} Y_\theta = \left(\frac{1}{1-\epsilon_1}\right) A.$$

Income, that is, would eventually reach the same stable level as in the multiplier model.

(ii) If q, the smaller root, exceeds unity then so does p, the larger root, and both Pp^θ and Qq^θ must increase as time goes on. It follows that y_θ goes on increasing, as in the un-lagged multiplier-accelerator model, although not usually at a steady rate. Income here grows steadily only in the exceptional case of $p=q$; then we would have

$$\frac{y_\theta}{y_{\theta-1}} - 1 = p - 1 = \frac{\epsilon_1 + \epsilon_2 - 2}{2}.$$

Even so, this growth rate is not the same as that in the unlagged model. In general, y has two components one of which grows at a steady rate of $p-1$ and the other at a steady rate of $q-1$, but they do not combine to give a steady rate for y. Its growth rate lies between $p-1$ and $q-1$ but increases towards $p-1$ if

$$q < p$$

and so

$$\underset{\theta \to \infty}{\text{Lim}}\ y_\theta = P p^\theta.$$

The other two possibilities occur if

$$(\epsilon_1 + \epsilon_2)^2 < 4\epsilon_2$$

so that we have to deal with the square root of a negative number. This requires us to move from the ordinary domain of real numbers to the less familiar domain of complex numbers which all involve,

$$i = \sqrt{-1}.$$

It looks queer but leads to useful results. The Appendix shows that, in our problem,

$$p = (\sqrt{\epsilon_2})\, e^{i\omega}$$
$$q = \sqrt{\epsilon_2})\, e^{-i\omega}$$

e being the usual exponential number, and ω being defined by the trigonometrical function

$$\cos \omega = \frac{\epsilon_1 + \epsilon_2}{2\sqrt{\epsilon_2}}.$$

We then obtain, as the Appendix shows, a solution

$$y_\theta = B\, (\sqrt{\epsilon_2})^\theta \cos (\theta\omega - \lambda)$$

where B and λ are constants depending on P and Q, and so on the initial value of y or Y.

The important point is that the solution is now neither a stable level of income nor a steadily growing income. Instead, there are cycles in income, and in its components, the cycles all having uniform period of $\dfrac{360}{\omega}$, i.e. this is the period from one peak or trough to the next. We can now set out the remaining two possibilities.

(iii) If p and q are complex numbers, and ϵ_2 is less than unity, then income undergoes regular but diminishing cycles and so eventually reaches the same stable level as in the multiplier model, $\left(\dfrac{1}{1-\epsilon_1}\right) A$.

(iv) If p and q are complex numbers, but ϵ_2 exceeds unity, then income undergoes increasing or explosive cycles which swing its peaks or troughs further and further away from an average level of $\left(\dfrac{1}{1-\epsilon_1}\right) A$.

The four possibilities may be represented graphically for periods following an increase in autonomous expenditures.

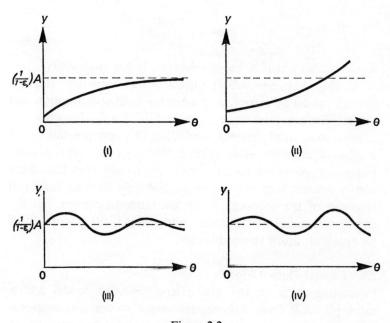

Figure 2.2

A famous example of a lagged multiplier-accelerator model is that associated with Hicks and Samuelson, viz.

$$Y_\theta = C_\theta + I_\theta + A$$
$$C_\theta = c Y_{\theta-1}$$
$$I_\theta = a (Y_{\theta-1} - Y_{\theta-2}).$$

It has the solution

$$Y_\theta = \left(\frac{1}{1-c}\right) A + Pp^\theta + Qq^\theta$$
$$2p = (c+a) + \sqrt{(c+a)^2 - 4a}$$
$$2q = (c+a) - \sqrt{(c+a)^2 - 4a}$$

and if

$$(c+a)^2 < 4a$$

the solution becomes oscillatory;

$$Y_\theta = \left(\frac{1}{1-c}\right) A + B (\sqrt{a}) \cos (\omega\theta - \lambda)$$

$$\cos \omega = \frac{c+a}{2\sqrt{a}}.$$

Cycles damp out if a, the accelerator, is less than unity.

As the Hicks-Samuelson model differs from the Harrod-Domar model by introducing a lag for both consumption and investment, yet gives three other possibilities for behaviour of income than steady growth, including two new possibilities of cyclical fluctuation, it is evident that lags can play a most important role in macro-economics. We should never take them lightly because they may influence, not only the time for a full response of the economy to an autonomous change, but the way it responds to that change and, indeed, the possibility of an eventual return to equilibrium.

2.6 Capital-Output Models

Interesting as it is, the multiplier-accelerator model has a more plausible rival. The capital-output model also supposes that a rise of income stimulates consumption and investment

32

but recognizes that investment can be checked by growth of capital. The reasoning here is that increasing national income stimulates demand for output and so raises profits. Higher profits both stimulate demand for investment and help to finance it but, owing to the tendency for diminishing returns from a relatively increasing factor of production, the stimulus becomes weaker as investment increases the stock of capital. Or, to put the last point in another way, the nearer output already is to the capacity limit set by existing capital equipment, the more strongly will rising profits stimulate further investment in such equipment.

An expression of this model may be given in which we again recognize the somewhat neglected influences of government spending, taxes or transfers, and also a uniform lag of consumption and investment behind income. It is:

(1) $$Y_\theta = C_\theta + I_\theta + G$$

(2) $$C_\theta = c \left(\frac{1 - t_d}{1 + t_i}\right) Y_{\theta - 1} = \gamma Y_{\theta - 1}$$

(3) $$I_\theta = i \left(\frac{1 - t_d}{1 + t_i}\right) Y_{\theta - 1} - \beta K_{\theta - 1} = a Y_{\theta - 1} - \beta K_{\theta - 1},$$

where K denotes capital and, by definition,

(4) $$I_\theta = K_\theta - K_{\theta - 1}.$$

From (1), (2) and (4) we derive

(5) $$Y_\theta = \gamma Y_{\theta - 1} + K_\theta - K_{\theta - 1} + G$$

and from (3) and (4)

(6) $$Y_{\theta - 1} = \left(\frac{1}{a}\right) K_\theta - \left(\frac{1 - \beta}{a}\right) K_{\theta - 1}$$

or

$$Y_\theta = \left(\frac{1}{a}\right) K_{\theta + 1} - \left(\frac{1 - \beta}{a}\right) K_\theta.$$

Substituting next (6) into (5) we find that

$$\left(\frac{1}{a}\right) K_{\theta+1} - \left(\frac{1-\beta}{a}\right) K_\theta = \left(\frac{\gamma}{a}\right) K_\theta - \gamma \left(\frac{1-\beta}{a}\right) K_{\theta-1} + K_\theta - K_{\theta-1} + G$$

and so obtain

(7) $\qquad K_{\theta+1} - (1+a-\beta+\gamma) K_\theta + (a-\beta\gamma+\gamma) K_{\theta-1} = aG$

or $\qquad K_\theta - (1+a-\beta+\gamma) K_{\theta-1} + (a-\beta\gamma+\gamma) K_{\theta-2} = aG.$

This is a second order linear difference equation in K, instead of in Y as for the lagged multiplier-accelerator model. The solution, in view of our preceding discussion[1], is

(8) $\qquad\qquad K_\theta = \left[\frac{a}{\beta (1-\gamma)}\right] G + Pp^\theta + Qq^\theta$

where

$$P + Q = k_0 = K_0 - \left[\frac{a}{\beta (1-\gamma)}\right] G.$$

$$2p = (1+a-\beta+\gamma) + h$$

$$2q = (1+a-\beta+\gamma) - h$$

$$h = \sqrt{(1+a-\beta+\gamma)^2 - 4(a-\beta\gamma+\gamma)}.$$

Again there are four possible modes of behaviour:

(i) If $(1+a-\beta+\gamma)^2 > 4(a-\beta\gamma+\gamma)$ and $p < 1$ then capital converges steadily to the stable level $\left[\dfrac{a}{\beta (1-\gamma)}\right] G$.

(ii) If $(1+a-\beta+\gamma)^2 > 4(a-\beta\gamma+\gamma)$ and $q > 1$ then K grows at an increasing rate which converges to $p - 1$.

(iii) If $(1+a-\beta+\gamma)^2 < 4(a-\beta\gamma+\gamma)$ and $(a-\beta\gamma+\gamma) < 1$ then K undergoes diminishing cycles to reach the stable level $\left[\dfrac{a}{\beta (1-\gamma)}\right] G$.

[1] The coefficient for G is obtained from equation (7) by putting $K_\theta = K_{\theta-1} = K_{\theta-2}$ to get stationary values of K.

34

(iv) If $(1+a-\beta+\gamma)^2 < 4\,(a-\beta\gamma+\gamma)$ and $(a-\beta\gamma+\gamma) > 1$ then K undergoes explosive cycles which carry its peaks or troughs further away from a mean level $\left[\dfrac{a}{\beta\,(1-\gamma)}\right]\,G$.

There are exactly similar possibilities for income or any of its components. We can see this by substituting (8) into (6) so as to obtain

$$aY_\theta = K_{\theta+1} - (1-\beta)\,K_{\theta-1} = \left(\dfrac{a}{1-\gamma}\right)\,G + P\,[p-(1-\beta)]\,p^\theta$$
$$+ Q\,[q-(1-\beta)]\,q^\theta,$$

i.e.

$$(9)\quad Y_\theta = \left(\dfrac{1}{1-\gamma}\right)\,G + Mp^\theta + Nq^\theta$$

$$M = \left(\dfrac{p+\beta-1}{a}\right)P$$

$$N = \left(\dfrac{q+\beta-1}{a}\right)Q.$$

2.7 Which is Best?

It appears that, even if the capital-output model makes a more plausible assumption about investment, it does not, in the end, differ much from the lagged multiplier-accelerator model. Both seem unsatisfactory if only because they lead either to growth or to regular cycles about a stationary level, whereas the real world shows irregular cycles about a rising trend of income, at least in advanced countries. Another difficulty is to believe that the possibility of explosive cycles is a real one.

The first difficulty could be removed by complicating the model. Cycles are made irregular by introducing random elements into models, and cycles about a trend become a possibility if we add an assumption that there is a trend in autonomous expenditures, A or G, or else introduce more complex lags extending over at least three periods of time.

But the second difficulty disappears only if the parameters in the models have certain critical values. Consider the multiplier-accelerator model; it excludes explosive oscillations only if a, the accelerator or capital-output ratio, is less than unity. This is certainly a wrong assumption in any advanced country, because there the stock of existing capital assets is 2–3 times the national income. The capital-output model, on the other hand, has damped cycles if, as we have just seen,

$$\gamma + a - \beta\gamma = \gamma(1-\beta) + a < 1.$$

This is by no means unlikely as γ, a and β are all bound to be less than unity and γ is much greater than a or β. Stability in the corresponding simple multiplier model would require the stronger condition $\gamma + a < 1$.

For these reasons the lagged capital-output model is more plausible than the multiplier-accelerator model, and superior to the multiplier model in allowing for both growth and fluctuation of income. The simple version here should be complicated to allow for fluctuation about a growth trend of income, and for rregularity of fluctuation through random or other influences, but there is no great difficulty about that.

Both accelerator and capital-output models, however, have a serious defect. In so far as they lead to fluctuations they suppose that the stock of capital is increased in an upswing and correspondingly decreased in a downswing. It is not unreasonable to suppose such behaviour for inventories, which can run down quickly, but it is contrary to commonsense and to experience to suppose that, if income falls off cyclically, capital equipment will be similarly reduced. It will be held idle temporarily rather than destroyed, only to be replaced by new equipment once the upswing begins. Some economists, such as Hicks and Goodwin, have thus used lop-sided accelerator models that limit reductions of capital equipment in downswings to normal wearing out through failure to provide for depreciation.

The three basic models by no means exhaust the possibilities of macro-economic theory. They provide, however, a preliminary view of its nature and power, and a useful framework of reference for discussing empirical work in macroeconomics.

Appendix

Linear Difference Equations

An n-th order linear difference equation has the form

$$Y_\theta + \sum_{r=1}^{n} a_r Y_{\theta-r} = \phi[\theta]. \qquad (1)$$

It has a solution of two components; a general solution of the homogeneous form

$$y_\theta + \sum_{r=1}^{n} a_r y_{r-\theta} = 0 \qquad (2)$$

and a particular solution of a trend or equilibrium equation

$$\bar{Y}_\theta = \bar{Y}[\theta]. \qquad (3)$$

The solution of (2) is found by putting

$$y_\theta = x^n \qquad (4)$$

and obtaining the auxiliary equation

$$x^n + \sum_{r=1}^{n} a_r x^{n-r} = 0. \qquad (5)$$

This polynomial has n roots, $p_1, p_2, ..., p_n$, not necessarily all different, each of which is a solution of (5) and hence of (2); i.e.

$$p_s^\theta + \sum_r a_r p_s^{\theta-r} = 0. \qquad (6)$$

But then

$$y_\theta = \sum_{s=1}^{n} P_s p_s^\theta \qquad (7)$$

is also a solution of (2) as may be verified by substitution, viz.

$$\sum_{s=1}^{n} P_s p_s^\theta + \sum_{r=1}^{n} a_r \sum_{s=1}^{n} P_s p_s^{\theta-r} = \sum_s P_s [p_s^\theta + \sum_r a_r p_s^{\theta-r}] = 0 \qquad (8)$$

in view of (6).

All roots of the auxiliary equation need not be real, and, if not, they must occur in conjugate-complex pairs, e.g.

$$p_1 = re^{i\omega} = r\,[\cos \omega + i \sin \omega] \qquad (9)$$
$$p_2 = re^{-i\omega} = r\,[\cos \omega - i \sin \omega]$$
$$r^2 = p_1 p_2, \cos \qquad \omega = \frac{p_1 + p_2}{2r}.$$

It follows, from (7) and (9) that, for such a pair

$$P_1 p_1^{\theta} + P_2 p_2^{\theta} = P_1 r^{\theta}\,[\cos \theta\omega + i \sin \theta\omega] + P_2 r^{\theta}\,[\cos \theta\omega - i \sin \theta\omega]$$

i.e.

$$P_1 p^{\theta} + P_2 p_2^{\theta} = r^{\theta}\{[P_1 + p_2] \cos \theta\omega + i\,[P_1 - P_2] \sin \theta\omega\}. \qquad (10)$$

Next define

$$P_1 + P_2 = B \cos \lambda = B_1 \qquad (11)$$
$$i\,(P_1 - P_2) = B \sin \lambda = B_2$$

so that

$$B_1{}^2 + B_2{}^2 = B^2\,(\cos {}^2\lambda + \sin {}^2\lambda) = B^2. \qquad (12)$$

It follows then that

$$P_1 p_1^{\theta} + P_2 p_2^{\theta} = Br^{\theta}\,(\cos \lambda \cos \theta\omega + \sin \lambda \sin \theta\omega)$$

i.e.

$$P_1 p_1^{\theta} + P_2 p_2^{\theta} = Br^{\theta} \cos (\theta\omega - \lambda). \qquad (13)$$

To each pair of conjugate-complex roots there thus corresponds a particular cycle about the trend or trends given by real roots.

It remains to find the particular solution which, when added to the general homogeneous solution, gives a complete solution of the difference equation. Here everything depends upon $\phi\,[\theta]$. If this is simply a constant, A, we have

$$\bar{Y}\,(\theta) = \frac{A}{1 + \Sigma a_r}. \qquad (14a)$$

But if $\phi\,[\theta]$ is a trend, Ab^{θ}, then

$$\bar{Y}\,(\theta) = \frac{Ab^{n+\theta}}{b^n + \Sigma a_r b^{n-r}}. \qquad (14b)$$

To prove this result we use the shift operator, E^r, which, applied to Y, gives

$$E^{-r} Y_{\theta} = Y_{\theta-r}, \; E^0 Y_{\theta} = Y_{\theta}$$

38

and when applied to (1) gives

$$(E^0 + \sum_{r=1}^{n} a_r E^{-r})\ \bar{Y}_\theta = Ab^\theta.$$

Hence we can have

$$(E^n + \sum_{r=1}^{n} a_r E^{n-r})\ \bar{Y}_\theta = AE^n b^\theta$$

or

$$\bar{Y}(\theta) = \frac{Ab^{n+\theta}}{b^n + \sum_{r=1}^{n} a_r b^{n-r}}.$$

The particular solution, therefore, is also a trend in this case. Other possibilities, of course, exist for $\phi\ [\theta]$ and no general statement can be made regarding their effect on the solution.

References

All topics discussed in this chapter are covered by
R. G. D. Allen, *Mathematical Analysis for Economists*, Chs. 2–7 and 20.
The fullest treatment of the aggregation problem is given by
H. Theil, *Linear Aggregation in Economic Relations*.
Models are fully treated by
A. R. Bergstrom, *The Construction and Use of Economic Models*, and, in a more elementary way, by
J. Tinbergen, *Economic Policy*.
See also
R. C. O. Matthews, *The Trade Cycle*.
Linear difference equations are explained in many texts; e.g.
W. J. Baumol, *Economic Dynamics*, Chs. 9–11;
C. V. Durell and A. Robson, *Advanced Algebra*, Ch. 11;
J. P. Lewis, *Mathematics for Students of Economics*, Ch. XXVI.

CHAPTER 3

A Note on Econometric Tests

Economics is a science in the sense that its theories have to be empirically tested. Theories which are flatly contradicted by facts have, of course, to be discarded. But flat contradiction is a limiting case, especially for theories which, like those of economics, are probabilistic rather than categorical statements. The more usual position is that we have to choose between alternative theories, none of which has yet been decisively refuted, according to better or worse agreement with the facts which they purport to explain.

Macro-economics, as Chapter 2.1 stressed, has peculiar and constant need of such testing because its inevitably loose or approximate character must leave open possibilities of error and of alternative explanations. We have, accordingly, always to look hard for, and at, alternative explanations with a view to discarding those which appear least satisfactory. These explanations, unfortunately, can seldom be tested by any simple or direct appeal to facts because they typically involve a somewhat complex relation between a number of different variables whose separate influences cannot be isolated by experimental methods, such as the natural sciences use.

We have, instead, to consider statistical estimates of macro-economic equations, or models, and a main reason for putting the theory into a mathematical form is precisely to help statistical testing of its worth. No adequate account of such testing can be attempted here, as that is the province of a difficult branch of our science known as 'econometrics'. Yet, if we are to interpret econometric equations for macro-economic relations, frequently quoted in later chapters, some guidance is needed.

Consider a variable, X, which, it is thought, might be explained by the n variables, $Z_1, Z_2, ..., Z_n$. A statistical test of the explanation requires a list of jointly recorded values of X and all the Z. This might be obtained for the same area or group over T successive periods of time ('time series'),

$$
\begin{array}{llll}
X_\theta & Z_{1,\,\theta} & Z_{2,\,\theta} & \ldots & Z_{n,\,\theta} \\
X_{\theta+1} & Z_{1,\,\theta+1} & Z_{2,\,\theta+1} & \ldots & Z_{n,\,\theta+1} \\
\multicolumn{5}{c}{\dotfill} \\
X_{\theta+T} & Z_{1,\,\theta+T} & Z_{2,\,\theta+T} & \ldots & Z_{n,\,\theta+T}
\end{array}
$$

or else for different areas or groups at about the same time (cross-section data),

$$
\begin{array}{llll}
X_\alpha & Z_{1,\,\alpha} & Z_{2,\,\alpha} & \ldots & Z_{n,\,\alpha} \\
X_\beta & Z_{1,\,\beta} & Z_{2,\,\beta} & \ldots & Z_{n,\,\beta} \\
\multicolumn{5}{c}{\dotfill} \\
X_\omega & Z_{1,\,\omega} & Z_{2,\,\omega} & \ldots & Z_{n,\,\omega}
\end{array}
$$

If such a record is available the econometrician can apply *regression analysis* to the jointly observed values of the variables so as to obtain an econometric equation having always the linear form

$$\hat{X} = \hat{A} + \hat{a}_1 Z_1 + \hat{a}_2 Z_2 + ... + \hat{a}_n Z_n.$$
$$(s_1) \qquad (s_2) \qquad\qquad (s_n)$$

Here the circumflexes denote estimates, and the bracketed s *standard errors* of the regression coefficients. There is also a *residual error*, e, between actual and estimated values of X,

$$e = X - \hat{X} = X - (\hat{A} + \hat{a}_1 Z_1 + \hat{a}_2 Z_2 + ... + \hat{a}_n Z_n).$$

Four points may be noted about the possibility of damagingly large residual errors.

(a) Regression analysis, for technical reasons, can yield only a linear equation, and hence a satisfactory estimate of X, only

41

if the corresponding theoretical relation is (or can be made) sufficiently linear, so that

$$X = A + a_1 Z_1 + a_2 Z_2 + \ldots + a_n Z_n + u$$

where u represents non-systematic, random or stochastic influences upon X.

(b) If u is so strong, relatively to a_1, a_2, ..., a_n, that X is overwhelmingly exposed to chance influences there is no hope of any good systematic explanation.

(c) If the Z omit variables needed for a proper explanation of X, then e will be greater than it should be and the regression equation unsatisfactory.

(d) Faulty measurement of X or the Z may also result in excessively high e.

Statistical testing can do little about the first difficulty and economic theory nothing about the second. But we can always try to find neglected explanatory variables or to improve measurement.

High residual errors thus point to an unsatisfactory explanation, but it is desirable to give precision to this idea. Such precision is supposed to be given by the *multiple correlation coefficient*, R, a test of association or covariation between X and $\hat{X}$; it may be defined as

$$R^2 = 1 - \frac{\Sigma e^2}{\Sigma (X - \bar{X})^2}$$

where $\bar{X}$ is the arithmetic mean of the recorded values of X. It can be shown that, if the estimates have been obtained by a particular kind of regression analysis known as the 'least squares' method, the value of R must be between unity, for perfect association, and zero for no association. The least squares method, however, is appropriate only for estimating a single, isolated equation. For equations which are part of a model ('simultaneous' equations) other methods of regression analysis are more appropriate; but then the above formula for R has no definite limits and hence is of little use for judging the worth of econometric equations yielded by these methods.

There is a further measure of correlation based upon e. It is called a measure of *serial correlation* and is given by the Durbin-Watson statistic,

$$d = \frac{\sum\limits_{\theta=2}^{T} (e_\theta - e_{\theta-1})^2}{\sum\limits_{\theta=1}^{T} (e_\theta)^2}.$$

It indicates the degree to which there is a systematic connection between successive values of the residual error. If there is such a connection this points to the need for finding a missing explanatory variable.

Serial correlation is strongly suspected when d falls below a lower limit d_l, and rejected only if it exceeds an upper limit, d_u. Tables for d_l and d_u have been worked out for various numbers of joint records of the variables and for various numbers of the explanatory variables, Z; for 20 joint records and 5 explanatory variables $d_l = 0.79$ and $d_u = 1.99$. Strictly speaking, however, the test assumes that e is a random number, conforming to the 'normal' distribution so dear to statisticians. The assumption does not hold generally for other methods of regression than least squares so that, in their case, the test is often inexact.

We pass from methods for judging agreement between a theoretical and an empirical equation to a more piece-meal method for judging whether or not a particular Z, say Z_r, has a systematic influence upon X. A rough rule here is to accept that Z_r does have a significant influence upon X only if $\hat{a}_r > 2s_r$; for then it may be shown, on reasonable probability assumptions, that we would have less than a 5 per cent chance of being wrong if, in truth, there were no systematic relation between Z_r and X. A stricter version of the rule is that $\hat{a}_r > 3s_r$ which would reduce our chance of a wrong decision from less than 5 per cent to less than 1 per cent. Econometricians thus speak of a 5 per cent, or a 1 per cent, 'significance' level for such a test.

It would require an excursion into statistical theory even to explain this rule. Here we need notice only two points. The more important is that the test is unreliable if the residual error

43

has a marked serial correlation. The other is that this test is also based upon the assumptions for least squares regression and thus holds only approximately in the case of other regression methods.

Suppose that a regression equation passes all these tests – that it has low residual error, little or no serial correlation of this error, and all regression coefficients are two or three times their own standard errors. We could then hold that the corresponding theoretical explanation has not been refuted by econometric tests and, if it passed the tests better than any alternative explanation, we could provisionally accept it. We could furthermore use the regression for deciding the comparative strength of influences from different Z upon X, an important matter about which theory has often to be vague.

Some caution is needed here. We can make *absolute* comparisons only if X and the Z are all measured in the same units. If, for example, we had

$$X = 0 \cdot 10 \, Z_1 + 0 \cdot 20 \, Z_2$$

where X represents investment, Z_1 consumption and Z_2 business profits, all measured in \$ million, then we could say that profits had twice the influence upon investment that consumption had. But what if, instead,

$$X = 0 \cdot 08 Z_1 + 0 \cdot 12 Z_2 - 0 \cdot 15 Z_3 - 0 \cdot 02 Z_4$$

where Z_3 represents the price of machinery and Z_4 the market rate of interest? No common unit of measurement now exists, and we can compare only *relative* influences. We should, that is, have to break free from different units of measurement and consider what percentage changes in X result from the same percentage change in the different Z. The relative influence of Z_1 upon X is (approximately)

$$\frac{percentage\ change\ in\ X}{percentage\ change\ in\ Z_1} = \frac{\Delta X}{X} \bigg/ \frac{\Delta Z_1}{Z_1} = \hat{a}_1 \frac{\bar{Z}_1}{X} = 0.08 \frac{\bar{Z}_1}{X}$$

where $\bar{X}$ and $\bar{Z}$ represent mean values of X and Z_1. Similarly we should express the relative influence of Z_2, Z_3 and Z_4 by

$$\hat{a}_2 \frac{\bar{Z}_2}{\bar{X}},\ \hat{a}_3 \frac{\bar{Z}_3}{\bar{X}}\ \text{and}\ \hat{a}_4 \frac{\bar{Z}_4}{\bar{X}};\ \text{i.e.}\ 0{\cdot}12 \frac{\bar{Z}_2}{\bar{X}},\ -0.15 \frac{\bar{Z}_3}{\bar{X}}\ \text{and}\ -0{\cdot}02 \frac{\bar{Z}_4}{\bar{X}}.$$

These relative influences are directly comparable.

It is seldom that econometric results are presented together with the averages required for such a comparison. We might be able to go to the original data in order to calculate them; failing that we can only make more or less informed guesses about their ratios.

References

C. Christ, *Econometric Methods and Models*, Ch. X.
J. Johnston, *Econometric Methods*, Ch. 4.
L. Klein, *Econometrics*, Ch. III.
E. Malinvaud, *Statistical Methods of Econometrics*, Ch. 6.

Part Two

Empirical Functions and Models

CHAPTER 4

Private Consumption

4.1 The Propensity to Consume

The simple form of consumption function used in the models of Chapter 2 was suggested by Keynes,[1] who held that real consumption tended to increase with disposable real income but by a smaller amount. He regarded interest as having little direct influence upon consumption, although he thought it might have an indirect effect by causing windfall changes in the value of financial assets or wealth. His followers, Clark[2] and Stone,[3] soon found statistical support for Keynes's consumption function:

$$C = C^* + cY_d.$$

Meanwhile Tinbergen had independently reached a similar function.[4] Statistical evidence led him to reject the idea that interest had any influence, direct or indirect, upon consumption, but he allowed for an influence from changes in the distribution of income by distinguishing workers' from capitalists' consumption, and he also allowed for a time lag in adjusting consumption to income. Workers, he thought, consumed all their disposable income, W, so that saving came only from profits, R, i.e.

$$C_\theta = C^* + W_\theta + cR_{\theta-1}.$$

[1] *The General Theory of Employment, Interest and Money*, (1935), Book III.

[2] *National Income and Outlay*, (1938), Ch. V.

[3] *Review of Economic Studies*, October 1938.

[4] 'An Economic Policy for 1936', republished in *Selected Economic Papers*, (1959).

But sometimes he took profits as depending upon aggregate expenditure or income so then

$$R_\theta = \rho Y_\theta$$

and, as

$$Y_\theta = W_\theta + R_\theta,$$

it followed that

$$C_\theta = C^* + (1 - \rho) Y_\theta + c\rho Y_{\theta-1} = C^* + c_1 Y_\theta + c_2 Y_{\theta-1}.$$

Some years later Brown[1] also stressed the influence of psychological inertia in adjusting consumption to income, but related this to previous consumption instead of to previous income; i.e.

$$C_\theta = C^* + c_1 Y_\theta + c_2 C_{\theta-1}.$$

After making his own statistical investigations of the problem, Klein[2] came to accept and place much reliance upon this type of hypothesis.

4.2 The Relative and Permanent Income Hypotheses

Consumption functions of the above sort would lead us to expect considerable *year-to-year* variations in the ratio of consumption or saving to income as income itself fluctuated. This expectation is, of course, borne out by annual national income accounts. Kuznets, however, found that there was little change, between 1869 and 1929, in the ratio of *decade averages* of saving and income.[3]

Duesenberry puzzled over this discrepant behaviour of the short-term and long-term ratios of saving to income.[4] He decided that they could be reconciled by a *relative income hypothesis* which made consumption depend, not only upon current income, but also upon maximum income to date. The basis for this idea is the argument that people are largely influenced by keeping up appearances, which depend upon their

[1] *Econometrica*, 1952.

[2] *Post-Keynesian Economics* (edited by K. Kurihara), 1955, pp. 289–98.

[3] *Uses of National Income in Peace and War*, (1942).

[4] *Income, Saving and Consumer Behaviour*, (1949).

consumption, so that if their income falls they will try to maintain consumption at the expense of saving. His function may be written as:

$$\frac{C_\theta}{Y_\theta} = c_1 - c_2 \left(\frac{Y_\theta}{Y_{max}} \right)$$

which becomes, if income is steadily rising so that $Y_\theta = Y_{max}$,

$$C_\theta = (c_1 - c_2) \ Y_\theta = c \ Y_\theta.$$

Since decade averages of income were rising from 1869 to 1929, this last equation could explain Kuznet's findings. But if income falls the ratio would rise, implying that consumption falls at a slower rate than income. Duesenberry speaks of this as a 'ratchet effect', which helps to stabilize the economy against short-term fluctuations of income arising from other causes.

Modigliani[1] reached a similar formula:

$$C_\theta = c_1 Y_\theta - c_2 \ (Y_\theta - Y_{max}) = (c_1 - c_2) \ Y_\theta + c_2 Y_{max}$$

but gave a different explanation. He stressed not only keeping up appearances but also inertia and changes in the distribution of income as income fluctuates.

More recently Friedman has advanced a theory that consumption depends, not on current or *measured* income, but upon expected or *permanent* income.[2] Consumption, that is, depends upon what people think they can afford to spend regularly, taking account of present assets, future earning power and short-term fluctuations of yearly income. Modigliani and Brumberg developed a similar idea about the same time.[3] As Friedman himself suggests, this permanent income hypothesis would coincide with the relative income hypothesis if permanent income could be interpreted as an average of current and maximum income, i.e. if

$$Y_\theta^P = a Y_\theta + (1 - a) \ Y_{max}$$

[1] *Conference on Income and Wealth*, Vol. 11, Pt. V.
[2] *A Study of the Consumption Function*, (1957).
[3] See *Post-Keynesian Economics*, Ch. 15.

51

because then Friedman's function

$$C_\theta = c Y_\theta^P$$

becomes

$$C_\theta = (ca) \, Y_\theta + c \, (1-a) \, Y_{max}$$

which has the same form as Modigliani's equation.

Klein,[1] however, has shown that if permanent income is more reasonably interpreted as a weighted average of past income and if, plausibly, the weights decrease in geometric proportion from the current period, then Friedman's formula would coincide with Brown's, i.e. if

$$C_\theta = c Y_\theta^P$$
$$Y_\theta^P = a Y_\theta + ab Y_{\theta-1} + ab^2 Y_{\theta-2} + ab^3 Y_{\theta-3} + \cdots$$

and

$$1 = a \, (1 + b + b^2 + b^3 + \cdots) = \frac{a}{1-b}$$

then it may be shown[2] that

$$C_\theta = ac Y_\theta + b C_{\theta-1} = c_1 Y_\theta + c_2 C_{\theta-1}.$$

Brown's formula thus appears to have merits unsuspected by its author. It can make reasonable allowance for the permanent income hypothesis and so reflects, in a way, the relative income hypothesis, too. Friedman,[3] in fact, acknowledges that it can be an approximation to his own hypothesis, and Duesenberry[4] says it gives just as satisfactory results as the relative income hypothesis.

4.3 The Influence of Income Distribution

Tinbergen allowed for the influence of changes in the distribution of income by giving separate marginal propensities to consume for workers and for capitalists. His estimates were

---

[1] *Journal of Political Economy*, 1958.
[2] The proof is as follows:
$$C_\theta = ac(Y_\theta + b Y_{\theta-1} + b^2 Y_{\theta-3} + \cdots)$$
$$b C_{\theta-1} = ac(b Y_{\theta-1} + b^2 Y_{\theta-2} + b^3 Y_{\theta-3} + \cdots)$$
so that $\qquad C_\theta - b C_{\theta-1} = ac Y_\theta$
or $\qquad C_\theta = ac Y_\theta + b C_{\theta-1}$
[3] *Journal of Political Economy*, 1958.
[4] *Business Cycles and Economic Growth*, (1958), pp. 177–8.

revised by the Netherlands Central Planning Bureau to 0·85 for workers and 0·40 for other income recipients. Klein and Goldberger[1] have gone a little further than this by estimating, from the United States data, long-run marginal propensities to consume of 0·81 for workers, 0·51 for farmers and 0·60 for other groups.

There are, evidently, big differences in consumption or saving habits between such broad income groups. We may notice, however, that even large changes in the division of income between them may have a comparatively small effect upon the community's general marginal propensity to consume. Using the Klein-Goldberger estimates it can be found that:

(a) if income is equally divided between the three groups the general marginal propensity would be 0·64;

(b) if farmers' income rose by one-half and incomes of workers and other capitalists each fell by one-quarter, the general marginal propensity becomes 0·61;

(c) if farmers' incomes fell by two-fifths and incomes of the other two groups each rose by one-fifth, the general marginal propensity becomes 0·67.

These are extreme changes, but do not greatly affect the general propensity and hence the multiplier. On the other hand, even a small change in the multiplier can have a large *absolute* effect upon income.

It also appears that changes in the distribution of income between individuals have comparatively slight effects upon consumption. Bronfenbrenner, Yamane and Lee[2] examined this problem on the basis of a study made for the Federal Reserve Board in 1950, which showed that the marginal propensity to consume ranged from 90 per cent for people having incomes below $1,000 to 60 per cent for people having incomes above $7,500. It would seem that a more equal distribution should increase consumption, but the authors found any such effect to be relatively small. A 10 per cent adjustment of all incomes towards their average would have raised consumption by less

---

[1] *An Econometric Model of the United States, 1929–49.*

[2] *Review of Economics and Statistics*, 1955.

than 1 per cent, and even a 50 per cent adjustment would have raised it by less than $3\frac{1}{2}$ per cent. The explanation here is that the poor are so much more numerous than the rich – the same explanation as for the well-known result that a complete equalization of incomes would do little directly to raise the incomes of the working class.

4.4 The Influence of Interest or Liquidity

Keynes argued that interest has little direct influence upon saving or consumption; even in theory the influence is uncertain because, if higher interest induces some people, anxious for greater income or wealth, to save more it will make others, aiming at a fixed provision for old age or dependents, save less. Keynes did recognize a possible indirect influence of interest upon consumption through windfall capital gains. In practice, however, Klein has said, 'no econometrician has ever found a significant correlation between consumption and interest rates',[1] a result which tells against indirect as well as direct effects of interest changes.

We need not, however, reject the idea that wealth has an influence upon consumption because, on Klein's interpretation of the permanent income hypothesis, consumption would depend upon the past stream of income, which is akin to wealth. Some writers, following a suggestion of Pigou's,[2] have emphasized liquid wealth as having an independent influence upon consumption. Patinkin,[3] the leading exponent of this *real balance effect*, gives a consumption function of the form

$$C = c_1 Y + c_2 L$$

where L denotes liquidity or the real value of money balances.

Both Brown and Klein have found some confirmation of this idea. Brown's later consumption function for Canada is:

$$C_\theta = 0{\cdot}508 + 0{\cdot}520W_\theta + 0{\cdot}293R_\theta + 0{\cdot}341C_{\theta-1} + 0{\cdot}099L_{\theta-1}$$
$$(0{\cdot}075)\ (0{\cdot}087)\quad (0{\cdot}068)\quad (0{\cdot}060)\quad (0{\cdot}021)$$

[1] *The Keynesian Revolution*, (1950), p. 60.
[2] *Economic Journal*, 1943.
[3] *Post-Keynesian Economics*, Ch. 5.

and the Klein-Goldberger consumption function for the United States is:

$$C_\theta = -22\cdot26 + 0\cdot55W_\theta + 0\cdot34A_\theta + 0\cdot41\ (R_\theta - A_\theta) + 0\cdot26C_{\theta-1}$$
$$(9\cdot66)\ \ (0\cdot06)\ \ \ \ (0\cdot04)\ \ \ \ (0\cdot05)\ \ \ \ \ \ \ \ \ \ \ (0\cdot08)$$
$$+ 0\cdot07L_{\theta-1} + \text{a population term}$$
$$(0\cdot03)$$

where A denotes agricultural incomes.

It appears, however, that the statistical association between consumption and liquidity is neither very strong nor very reliable. As Klein points out, theory gives the same uncertain answer here as in the case of interest. When some people's liquid assets increase, their need for further saving will diminish if they aim at a more or less fixed future provision, but for others an increase of liquid assets may encourage more saving for investment in illiquid or riskier assets. Studies of family budgets seem to reflect this conflict.

In low income groups the effect of liquid assets on savings is significantly negative. As one moves up the income scale the effect is alternated and even reverses direction at higher income levels . . . On balance there is probably more strength to the negative than to the positive effect of wealth on saving.[1]

4.5 Recent Findings

Zellner[2] has used quarterly data for the United States, over the period 1947–55, to test a variety of consumption functions involving current and previous income, previous maximum income, previous consumption and previous liquid assets. Only two of these functions met statistical criteria of having co-efficients whose algebraic signs are consistent with theory, confidence intervals which exclude a zero value for regression coefficients and residuals which are not serially correlated. These two functions were:

$$C_\theta = -21\cdot91 + 0\cdot708\,Y_\theta + 0\cdot368L_{\theta-1}$$
$$(0\cdot021)\ \ \ \ (0\cdot054)$$

[1] *Post-Keynesian Economics*, p. 293.
[2] *Econometrica*, 1957.

and

$$C_\theta = -18\cdot96 + 0\cdot375\,Y_\theta + 0\cdot489C_{\theta-1} + 0\cdot219L_{\theta-1}$$
$$ (0\cdot110) \quad (0\cdot160) \quad\quad (0\cdot067)$$

They gave support to the view that previous holdings of liquid assets influenced present consumption, and pointed to a stronger influence from previous consumption than Klein and Goldberger had found. On the other hand, as Zellner points out, the long-run marginal propensity to consume (found by dividing the coefficient for income by one minus the coefficient for previous consumption) is only 0·73, which appears too low.

Suits, in a research study for the Commission on Money and Credit,[1] obtained a different result by using annual data from 1948 to 1959;

$$\Delta C_\theta = 0.528\Delta\,Y_\theta + 0\cdot549\Delta L_{\theta-1} - 0\cdot432\Delta C_{\theta-1} + 3\cdot984$$
$$ (0\cdot085) \quad\quad (0\cdot082) \quad\quad (0\cdot098)$$

This confirmed the influence of liquid assets but gave a quite unplausible negative influence for previous consumption. He found, however, that, on disaggregating consumption between automobiles, other durables, non-durables and services, negative coefficients for previous purchases occurred only in the case of automobiles and, to a much lesser extent, in that of other durables. He explains this by the idea that consumer durables are a form of capital, 'consumer capital', and, as the capital-output theory postulates in regard to business investment, the previous stock of capital tends to depress further spending on capital assets.

Griliches, Maddala, Lucas and Wallace[2] repeated Zellner's tests against revised data and for a somewhat longer period, 1947–60. The second of a set of satisfactory results was:

$$C_\theta = 13\cdot1 + 0\cdot539\,Y_\theta + 0\cdot265C_{\theta-1} + 0\cdot258L_{\theta-1}.$$
$$ (0\cdot077) \quad (0\cdot102) \quad\quad (0\cdot040)$$

Like Zellner, they found a significant positive coefficient for previous consumption, but a lower one. The corresponding

[1] *Impacts of Monetary Policy*, pp. 32–35.
[2] *Econometrica*, 1962.

56

estimate of the long-run marginal propensity to consume was 0·73, about the same as Zellner's and also too low. They suggest that this may be explained by liquid assets, which they also found had a marked influence, perhaps as a proxy variable for some aspect of permanent income. For a function omitting liquid assets, viz.

$$C_\theta = 0·300\,Y_\theta + 0·670C_{\theta-1} + 3·100$$
$$(0·085) \qquad (0·097)$$

they found a long-run marginal propensity of 0·91.

They also estimated a revised form of the relative income hypothesis which had been put forward by Duesenberry, Eckstein and Fromm.[1] Their estimate is

$$\frac{C_\theta}{Y_{\theta-1}} = 0·839 - \underset{(0·134)}{0·565}\,\frac{Y_\theta}{Y^{max}_{\theta-1}} + \underset{(0·099)}{0·705}\,\frac{C_{\theta-1}}{Y_{\theta-2}}$$

giving a long-run marginal propensity of 0·93. This estimate of the function, however, has a lower multiple coefficient of correlation than that of the authors ($R^2 = 0·533$ as against $R^2 = 0·866$), and somewhat different coefficients. Both teams found that the function gave poor results between 1958 and 1960.

4.6 Conclusions

Many possible influences upon private consumption have been suggested, and tests have been made to sort out their relative importance or unimportance. It is evident that the results of such econometric testing are fairly sensitive to the quality of available data. Progress here, as in other branches of macro-economics, depends very much upon that of social accounting.

All tests, however, show a weak influence from the rate of interest. They also show that current income, by itself, does not provide a complete explanation – that there are other influences upon private consumption. Findings about these other influences are by no means clear-cut but seem to point, in various ways, to the permanent income hypothesis or to some variant of it.

[1] *Econometrica*, 1960.

The strongest contender, here, is the influence of previous consumption which Friedman accepts is compatible with his hypothesis, as would be that of previous income, another strong contender. The evidence for an influence from holdings of liquid assets is perhaps weaker, if strengthened by recent studies based on quarterly data, and such an influence may also be compatible with the hypothesis, as would that of wealth. The influence of changes in the distribution of income is less evident but, unless there are large changes, seems unlikely to have much effect upon aggregate consumption.

CHAPTER 5

Private Investment

5.1 The Prospensity to Invest

Keynes had suggested that investment or capital formation depends mainly on the rate of interest, although he emphasized that this relation was rather unstable because it could change quickly and drastically with the 'state of long-term expectation'. In so far as expectation depends upon current or past income we should be inclined to say that investment depends upon income as well as upon interest, a conclusion early drawn by Hicks.[1] Keynesians thus soon began to talk of a *propensity to invest*, similar to the propensity to consume, so that the multiplier became not merely the reciprocal of the marginal propensity to save $\left(\dfrac{1}{s}\right)$ but the reciprocal of the difference between the marginal propensities to save and to invest, $\left(\dfrac{1}{s-i}\right)$.

Tinbergen reached a similar conclusion. But his, and other, statistical investigations led him to believe that interest had little or no influence upon aggregate investment, although it had some influence upon investment in assets having a long life and a fairly stable return; e.g. railroads, ships or houses.[2] This negative result seemed to be confirmed by a prewar Oxford inquiry[3] into business motives for investment, and by similar inquiries elsewhere. Finding that profits had the strongest single

[1] *Econometrica*, 1937.
[2] *Dynamics of Business Cycles*, pp. 163–82.
[3] *Oxford Studies in the Price Mechanism*, Ch. I.

influence, Tinbergen was led to formulate a *profit principle* for investment of the form:

$$I_\theta = I^* + iR_{\theta-1}.$$

A lag occurs, not only because of the time between accruals of profits and their distribution, but also because of the time needed to prepare investment plans and carry them out. Profits have a double role; they give an inducement to invest and provide part of the finance needed. Sometimes, however, Tinbergen is content with a looser statement of the propensity to invest; 'since fluctuations in national income run approximately parallel with fluctuations in profits . . . it may also be stated as a reasonable approximation that fluctuations in investment are largely determined by fluctuations in incomes'.[1] We should then have

$$I_\theta = I^* + iY_{\theta-1}$$

where i is the marginal propensity to invest.

5.2 The Pure Acceleration Principle and the Inventory Cycle

An alternative principle comes from the idea that an increase of production requires an increase of capital equipment. The simplest relation here would be one of proportionality, i.e.

$$K_\theta = aY_\theta$$

where a is called the *capital-output ratio*. Investment, being the current increase of capital, then depends not upon the *level* of income, as in the case of the propensity to invest, but upon the *increase* of income, i.e.

$$I_\theta = K_\theta - K_{\theta-1} = a\,(Y_\theta - Y_{\theta-1}).$$

In this context, a has been called the *accelerator*.

One important application of this principle is to explain investment in stocks or inventories. Tinbergen, and others, maintain that there is a 'pronounced tendency to keep stocks in proportion to the volume of sales'. He calls this a technical influence, but also recognizes a speculative influence from the desire to profit from expected changes in prices of stocks held

[1] *Dynamics of Business Cycles*, p. 172.

against sales, or to avoid loss from expected changes in prices of stocks held for productive purposes. The technical and the speculative influences both relate to desired or voluntary adjustment of stocks. There are also, however, undesired or involuntary changes arising from the role of stocks as a buffer or real reserve against unexpected changes in demand or supply.

We saw, in Chapter 2, that an acceleration principle might explain cyclical fluctuations of income. It will now be shown, by a model derived from Lundberg[1] and Metzler,[2] how this principle might, in particular, explain an inventory cycle, all too familiar in the United States. First, we take income as equal to planned output of consumption goods, $\bar{C}$, plus planned additions to inventories, $\bar{V}$, plus other production, here taken to be autonomous, A^*:

$$Y_\theta = \bar{C}_\theta + \bar{V}_\theta + A^*.$$

Planned output of consumer goods is supposed to equal previous sales,

$$\bar{C}_\theta = C_{\theta-1}$$

and actual sales to depend upon income,

$$C_\theta = c Y_\theta.$$

Planned additions to inventories equal planned inventories, $\bar{K}$, less previous actual inventories, $K_{\theta-1}$, i.e.

$$\bar{V}_\theta = \bar{K}_\theta - K_{\theta-1}.$$

Using Tinbergen's technical influence only, we take planned inventories to be fixed in proportion to planned sales,

$$\bar{K}_\theta = a\bar{C}_\theta$$

and to differ from actual inventories by unintended sales,

$$K_\theta = \bar{K}_\theta - (C_\theta - \bar{C}_\theta).$$

From these relations it is not hard to deduce that

$$Y_\theta = c\,(2+a)\,Y_{\theta-1} - c\,(1+a)\,Y_{\theta-2} + A^*.$$

[1] *Studies in the Theory of Economic Expansion*, (1937), Ch. IX.

[2] *Review of Economics and Statistics*, Vol. 23. See also R. G. D. Allen, *Mathematical Economics*, pp. 221–23.

Suppose that we have data for quarterly periods, that $c = 0.80$ and $a = 0.25$. Then the last equation becomes

$$Y_\theta = 1.8 Y_{\theta-1} - 1.0 Y_{\theta-2} + A*.$$

It implies steady cycles having a period of 14 quarters of $3\frac{1}{2}$ years, not far from the average of American inventory cycles.[1] Suppose, further, that income is initially stable at 1,000, and that initial equilibrium is disturbed by a rise of autonomous expenditures from 200 to 300. Subsequent developments are worked out, from the last equation, in the table opposite.

A good deal of econometric work has been done on inventory cycles, especially in the United States where they are a prominent feature of economic life. Darling[2] found, as had other investigators, that 'the acceleration principle is a powerful tool of economic analysis' in studying inventory fluctuations and, from quarterly data for manufacturing companies, 1947–58, he obtained the regression

$$V_\theta = -0.387 + 0.415 S_{\theta-1} - 0.212 K^v_{\theta-2} + 0.324 \Delta O_{\theta-1}$$
$$ (0.044) \phantom{S_{\theta-1}} (0.022) (0.054)$$

where S denotes sales and O new orders. Smith[3] updated this regression to 1961, finding

$$V_\theta = -0.038 + 0.327 S_{\theta-1} - 0.173 K^v_{\theta-2} + 0.149 \Delta O_{\theta-1}.$$

A disturbing feature of the two regressions is the very different estimate of an accelerator influence. But, as Eisner and Strotz say,[4] econometric studies of inventory investment, 'are all primitive and pioneering'.

---

[1] We have, from Appendix A,

$$\cos \theta = \frac{1.8}{2\sqrt{1.0}} = 0.9$$

therefore $\quad\quad\quad\quad \theta = 25.9$ degs.

so that the cycle has a period of

$$\frac{360}{25.9} = 13.9 \text{ quarters} = 3.48 \text{ years.}$$

[2] *American Economic Review*, 1959.
[3] Quoted, *Impacts of Monetary Policy*, p. 210.
[4] *Impacts of Monetary Policy*, p. 226.

Period (t)	Y	$=$	$\bar{C}$	$+$	$\bar{V}$	$+$	A^*
0	1,000		800		0		200
1	1,100		800		0		300
2	1,280		880		100		300
3	1,510		1,024		186		300
4	1,727		1,203		224 (P)		300
5	1,905		1,382		223		300
6	2,002 (P)		1,524		178		300
7	1,999		1,602 (P)		97		300
8	1,896		1,599		−3		300
9	1,714		1,517		−103		300
10	1,489		1,371		−182		300
11	1,266		1,191		−225 (T)		300
12	1,090		1,013		−223		300
13	996 (T)		872		−176		300
14	1,003		797 (T)		−94		300
15	1,109		802		7		300
16	1,293		887		106		300
17	1,518		1,034		184		300
18	1,739		1,214		225 (P)		300
19	1,912		1,391		221		300
20	2,003 (P)		1,530		173		300
21	1,993		1,602 (P)		91		300
22	1,884		1,594		−10		300
23	1,698		1,507		−109		300
24	1,472		1,358		−186		300
25	1,252		1,178		−226 (T)		300
26	1,082		1,002		−220		300
27	996 (T)		866		−170		300
28	1,011		797 (T)		−86		300

P denotes a peak and T a trough.

5.3 The Capacity Principle and Capital-Output Models

Even if the acceleration principle applies to investment in
stocks, which can rapidly decrease as income falls, it is difficult
to believe that it can apply to investment in fixed capital, which
is not rapidly scrapped during depressions although there may
be some decline through failure to replace fully depreciated
assets. Tinbergen pointed this out long ago, showing that the
acceleration principle worked badly in statistical explanations
of railways, shipping and cotton spinning.[1]

[1] *Economica*, 1938.

EMPIRICAL FUNCTIONS AND MODELS

Chenery[1] suggested a modified or flexible acceleration principle, called the *capacity principle*, which might reduce the objection. He relates, in effect, this type of investment, F, to the difference between utilization and capacity of equipment. Capacity output may be denoted $\tilde{Y}$, and taken to correspond to an 'optimum degree of utilization' of the preceding stock of equipment, i.e.

$$\tilde{Y}_\theta = nK_{\theta-1}.$$

Investment in fixed capital is taken to depend upon the gap between actual output and capacity output

$$F_\theta = b\,(Y_\theta - \tilde{Y}_\theta) = b\,Y_\theta - bnK_{\theta-1}.$$

Chenery tested his capacity principle against the ordinary accelerator principle for six American industries, finding that it gave better results for electricity, steel and zinc, but worse results for petrol refining and paper manufacture.

Klein and Goldberger[2] gave a similar statistical formula for private investment in the United States

$$F_\theta = -16\cdot7 + 0\cdot78R_\theta - 0\cdot07K_{\theta-1} + 0\cdot14L_{\theta-1}$$
$$(4\cdot7)\ (0\cdot18)\quad (0\cdot07)\quad\quad (0\cdot11)$$

although Klein originally derived the form of this equation from the theory of profit maximization.[3] Liquidity seems to

[1] *Econometrica*, 1952.

[2] L. R. Klein and A. S. Goldberger, *An Econometric Model of the United States, 1929–1949.*

[3] Net discounted profits from fixed investment, F, are to be maximized with respect to such investment but subject to the constraint of a Cobb-Douglas production function (where L denotes labour),

$$Y = L^l(K+F)^k,\ l+k=1.$$

It is assumed that the return from any given investment is constant over time and that the wage-bill, W, is also constant.

We have, then, for maximum profits from investment,

$$\frac{\partial}{(\partial K+F)}[(Y-W)\textstyle\int e^{-r\theta}.\,d\theta - F]\frac{d(K+F)}{dF} = 0$$

therefore

$$kY\textstyle\int e^{-r\theta}.\,d\theta - (K+F) = 0$$

and obtain, for assests having a very long life,

$$F = \left(\frac{k}{r}\right)Y - K.$$

See L. Klein, *The Keynesian Revolution*, pp. 196–9, and *Post-Keynesian Economics*, p. 296.

play a more definite, if somewhat uncertain role here, just as it does for consumption.

The Netherlands Central Planning Bureau[1] found a similar explanation of Dutch investment, but one which gives a stronger and more certain role to liquidity. Their formula is:

$$F_\theta = 2 \cdot 51 + 0 \cdot 78 R_\theta - 2 \cdot 55 U_\theta - 0 \cdot 49 P_\theta^k + 0 \cdot 63 L_{\theta-1}.$$
$$(2 \cdot 01) \ (0 \cdot 24) \quad (1 \cdot 41) \quad (0 \cdot 30) \quad (0 \cdot 19)$$

Here P^k denotes price of capital goods and U the percentage of the labour force that is unemployed. This percentage was used as an indirect index of the degree of non-utilization of capital equipment because satisfactory estimates of the capital stock were not available.

The capacity principle leads to the kind of capital-output model outlined in Chapter 2, where we saw that it could also explain cyclical fluctuations in fixed investment or income, and more plausibly than the pure accelerator principle. Such an explanation is used in two well-known models by Smithies[2] and Duesenberry[3] for the American economy.

5.4 Recent Findings

Meyer and Kuh[4] have made perhaps the most ambitious study of the determinants of fixed investment by cross-section analyses for different industries between 1946 and 1950. Their results are somewhat complex, but they found that internal liquidity (i.e. retained profits and depreciation funds) was of central importance, and that the acceleration principle worked well in 1946 and 1947 although its influence was more long- than short-run. Eisner,[5] in another cross-section study, for 1948–50, also found evidence of a lagged acceleration principle which, he claimed, accounted for about two-thirds of the adjustment of capital to output. (He found, too, a positive relation between

[1] P. J. Veerdoorn and C. J. van Eyk, *Experimental Short-Term Forecasting Models*, (1958), pp. 12–16.

[2] *Econometrica*, 1957.

[3] *Business Cycles and Economic Growth*, (1958).

[4] *The Investment Decision: An Empirical Study*, (1957).

[5] *Econometrica*, 1960.

fixed investment and profits.) Eisner and Strotz,[1] in their survey of empirical findings about fixed investment, stress sophisticated forms of the acceleration principle, as against the profit principle, and emphasize the uncertain influence of the rate of interest.

This last finding has been challenged by subsequent work of De Leeuw,[2] which Eckstein,[3] in extending it, hailed as breaking new ground by considering lags between investment *decisions* and expenditures. De Leeuw used quarterly data, from 1947 to 1959, in order to test a hypothesis that manufacturing investment in fixed capital, F, is related to capital requirements, Γ, taken as the difference between current output and 90 per cent of capacity output, internal funds, Φ, and the current yield of industrial bonds, r.

The hypothesis is interesting enough to be described even in a brief survey. De Leeuw first relates the above variables, not to current investment, but to a backlog of previously decided projects as this backlog is supposed to be continuously adjusted to capital requirements, internal funds and the interest which they could earn if invested outside the business. New projects are always being added to the backlog but it is also reduced by current investment. We thus have

increase of backlog = new projects − investment

or   new projects = increase of backlog + investment.

The crucial assumption is next made that current investment includes a definite proportion, k_j, of the projects that were added in any previous period, $\theta - j$. This means that

$$F_\theta = \sum_j k_j (\text{increase of backlog})_{\theta-j} + \Sigma k_j F_{\theta-j}$$

and, if the backlog is a linear function of Γ, Φ, and r, that

$$\tilde{F}_\theta \equiv F_\theta - \Sigma k_j F_{\theta-j} = f_1 \Delta \bar{\Gamma} + f_2 \Delta \Phi - f_3 \Delta \bar{r}.$$

where bars over the variables denote that they are weighted averages of past values.

De Leeuw investigated the effect of various types of lags in this general equation, and found that the best statistical results

[1] *Impacts of Monetary Policy.*

[2] *Econometrica*, 1962.

[3] *Econometrica*, 1965.

were obtained by using 'an inverted V' lag, i.e. one in which first half of the k's are proportional to the rising series, $1, 2, 3, ...,$ $\frac{\eta}{2}$, and the second half to the falling series, $\frac{\eta}{2}, \frac{\eta}{2} - 1, ..., 2, 1$. This means that initial effects on investment of a change in the backlog are small but build up to a maximum and thereafter steadily decline. The best value for η was found to be 12.

Eckstein extended this regression to 1950–62 without significantly affecting De Leeuw's results, viz.

$$\tilde{F} = -0{\cdot}617 + 0{\cdot}347\varDelta\bar{\varGamma} + 1{\cdot}226\varDelta\bar{\varPhi} - 4{\cdot}892\varDelta\bar{r}.$$
$$(0{\cdot}035) \quad (0{\cdot}594) \quad (0{\cdot}943)$$

This equation, besides confirming the capacity principle by finding a significant coefficient for $\varDelta\bar{\varGamma}$, also gives a significant influence from internal funds and, unlike most previous investigations, a significant influence from the rate of interest!

Eckstein made a further improvement by adding an 'expectational' variable, the ratio of unfilled orders to sales, which we may denote by ρ. He then found a regression equation which may be represented as

$$\tilde{F} = 0{\cdot}567 + 0{\cdot}279\varDelta\bar{\varGamma} + 0{\cdot}882\varDelta\bar{\varPhi} - 3{\cdot}715\varDelta\bar{r} + 19{\cdot}54\bar{\rho}.$$
$$(0{\cdot}024) \quad (0{\cdot}388) \quad (0{\cdot}604) \quad (3{\cdot}30)$$

The effect of this addition was to reduce the coefficients for all variables appearing in De Leeuw's regression, and to make that for the influence of internal funds statistically doubtful. But the capacity principle survives very well, and the influence of the interest rate is confirmed. It has, however, to be emphasized, that a significant influence from the bond yield was obtained by De Leeuw only in the case of the inverted V type of lag. When he tried other types of lag (rectangular or geometrically declining lags) statistical estimates of the coefficient for interest became unsatisfactory, as did those for the influence of internal funds. Only the capacity principle survived all tests of lags.

There is one economy where the influence of interest upon fixed investment emerges clearly enough without resort to close investigation of lags. In Japan, enterprises obtain much of their finance from banks and the central bank makes strong use of interest changes for controlling liquidity and hence aggregate demand. The official econometric model[1] for the medium-term economic plan, 1964–8, gives this equation for gross fixed private investment.

$$F_\theta = 1958 \cdot 4 + 2 \cdot 506 \left(\frac{R}{P_f}\right)_{\theta-1} - 799 \cdot 0 r_{\theta-1}$$
$$(0 \cdot 181) \qquad (389 \cdot 5)$$

where R denotes corporate income net of taxes and P_f the price of new fixed equipment. There is a corresponding equation for inventory investment,

$$V_\theta = 1914 \cdot 4 + 0 \cdot 351 Y_\theta^G - 0 \cdot 351 K_{\theta-1}^V - 956 \cdot 0 r_{\theta-1}.$$
$$(0 \cdot 069) \qquad (0 \cdot 069) \qquad (405 \cdot 2)$$

Although the influence of interest in both equations looks strong, the coefficients are not very reliable.

Postscript

At the proof reading stage of this book another important result has come to hand. Jorgenson and Stephenson (*Econometrica*, April, 1967) present a most important study of investment in US manufacturing for fifteen industries and the whole economy, using quarterly data for the period 1947–60. Their analysis, which is well supported by econometric results, ultimately makes such investment depend upon

(a) successive lagged values of first differences between ratios of output to a sophisticated index of the cost of capital services (including the rate of interest);

(b) successive first differences between previous net investment and replacement investment, the latter taken as proportional to the previous capital stock.

These results are thus consistent with a refined version of the capacity principle, and emphasize the importance of properly formulated lag relations.

[1] Economic Planning Agency, *Econometric Models for Medium-term Economic Plan, 1964–1968*, (1965), p. 25.

CHAPTER 6

Liquidity

6.1 Key Notions

Our survey of consumption and investment theories suggests that holdings of liquid balances have some influence upon both types of private spending and that the rate of interest may have an influence upon investment. It is an old idea, moreover, that there is some connection between available liquid balances and rates of interest. Although, then, liquidity does not appear among the variables in the social accounts, it may well influence the behaviour of these variables and, if so, there would be reason for believing that monetary authorities can do something to help regulate the aggregate demand for goods and services. The influence of fiscal policy was recognised in the models presented in Chapter 2. We have now to get some idea about the scope for monetary policy by considering the demand for liquidity. (Fuller consideration of the possibilities of both monetary and fiscal policy is given in later chapters.)

Liquidity means the real value of money balances held by the private sector; i.e. the quantity of money in circulation valued at constant prices. There are various definitions of what constitutes money in this connection, the chief contenders being a definition which includes only cash and cheque deposits, and another which also includes time and savings deposits. We shall use the symbols L to denote liquidity, M money (however defined), P the general level of prices as shown by an appropriate index, and r the market rate of interest. Our definitional relation is then

$$L = \frac{M}{P}.$$

Demand for liquid balances is for holdings of them, and so is a kind of inventory demand but one split between households and businesses. For households liquid balances are a type of durable consumer goods, and for businesses a type of productive asset needed for the smooth conduct of operations or transactions. Keynes[1] listed two motives for holding liquid balances that depend roughly upon the level of income, and one motive that depends largely upon the rate of interest. Both households and firms need a stock of money in order to bridge inevitable gaps between flows of receipts and expenditures and so to maintain a smooth flow of consumption or production; they also need such a stock in order to meet unexpected contingencies or to take advantage of unexpected bargains. He called these the *transactions* and *precautionary* motives, and held that both would tend to vary closely with income.

But he also emphasized a speculative motive for holding liquid balances. This relates to the choice between holding wealth, or accumulated savings, in the form either of money or of income-yielding assets such as property or securities. It suffices to consider securities which are the closest substitute for money as a 'store of value', to use an old-fashioned phrase. In order to understand such substitution we need to keep in mind the commercial formula for the price of a security and, for simplicity, take the case of a perpetual bond having a fixed nominal yield, i, on a nominal value, B, and quite riskless. Its price, p^b, is

$$p^b = \frac{i}{r}B.$$

The price of a bond thus varies inversely with the current market rate of interest.

Keynes thought that, as money and bonds are substitute means of holding wealth, and as substitution depends on relative prices or, in this case, upon the market rate of interest, then demand for liquidity must also depend upon the rate of interest, decreasing as interest rises and increasing as it falls. A crucial idea here is that people have a view about what is a

[1] *The General Theory of Employment, Interest and Money* (1935), Ch. 15.

'safe' level of bond prices, or a 'normal' level of interest rates. As bond prices rise, or interest rates fall, more and more people would feel that bond prices were more likely to fall than to rise, or that a rise of interest rates was more likely than a further fall. They would thus tend to switch from bonds to liquid assets. Conversely, as bond prices fell, or interest rates rose, there would be increasing expectations of future gain from buying securities now in order to resell them later at higher prices.

These ideas could be represented by a linear demand function for liquidity; i.e.

$$L = l_1 Y - l_2 r.$$

Keynes thought that the transactions and precautionary demands for liquidity were proportional to income but doubted whether the speculative demand was exactly inverse to the rate of interest. He feared, rather, that there might be some low level of interest rates, or some particularly high level of security prices, at which the demand for liquidity would become virtually insatiable. This, of course, is the famous 'liquidity trap', based on the view that the rate of interest cannot fall to anything like zero. The major reason for this belief is that expectations are not likely to be linear; rather, the expectation of a further rise in bond prices is likely to be less at a high than at a low level of these prices, and there will be some levels so high as to make everyone fear a future fall of bond prices and so attempt conversion of all securities into money. A subsidiary reason is that, as bond prices rise, the smaller becomes the insurance against a fall provided by the current yield of bonds. As Keynes pointed out, a market yield of 4 per cent compensates for a future rise of interest rates by 0·16 per cent a year, but a market yield of only 2 per cent for a future rise of only 0·04 per cent a year.[1]

If this view about the speculative demand for liquidity is accepted it would lead to a non-linear demand function such as

$$L = l_1 Y + \frac{l_2}{r - l_3}$$

showing that demand for liquidity becomes absolute as interest

---

[1] For if $p = \frac{i}{r} B$ then $\frac{dp^b}{dr} = -\frac{i}{r^2} B.$

approaches a minimum level represented by l_3. We shall see later that some important conclusions about the behaviour of the economy, and about the usefulness of monetary policy may turn upon this view of the speculative demand for liquidity and, in particular, on the idea of a liquidity trap setting a lower positive limit to the current market rate of interest.

6.2 Empirical Work

As early as 1939 A. J. Brown[1] estimated a statistical demand function for liquidity having a linear form. Tobin,[2] however, and others, found a non-linear dependence of liquidity demand upon the rate of interest. Klein,[3] at one time, considered that such evidence for a liquidity trap was unreliable owing to paucity of observations at very low rates of interest; but more recently, he and Goldberger[4] used a non-linear function for estimating household demand for liquidity in the United States.

An important testing of liquidity functions has been made by Bronfenbrenner and Mayer.[5] They obtained two estimates for total balances using data from the period 1919 to 1956;

$$\text{Log } L = 0\cdot1065 - 0\cdot0928 \text{ Log } r_s - 0\cdot1158 \text{ Log } K + 0\cdot7217 \text{ Log } L_{-1}$$
$$(0\cdot0139) \qquad (0\cdot0883) \qquad (0\cdot0576)$$
$$+ 0\cdot3440 \text{ Log } \tilde{Y}$$
$$(0\cdot0862)$$

where r_s is the short-term rate of interest, K national wealth and $\tilde{Y}$ gross national product less government consumption. This shows the expected direct dependence of liquidity demand upon income and its inverse dependence upon interest. The inclusion of wealth, and of previous liquidity, point to Friedman's permanent income hypothesis. But the authors emphasize that the coefficient for wealth is rather doubtful, and that L_{-1} may be interpreted as reflecting a supply relationship – 'the unwillingness

---

[1] Published in *Oxford Studies in the Price Mechanism*, (1951), edited by T. Wilson and P. W. S. Andrews; pp. 32–41.

[2] *Review of Economics and Statistics*, 1947.

[3] *The Keynesian Revolution*, p. 72.

[4] *An Econometric Model of the United States*.

[5] *Econometrica*, 1960.

of the monetary authority to permit sharp year-to-year changes in the money supply'. They accordingly recalculated the above equation omitting L_{-1}. The revised result was

$$\text{Log } L = 0{\cdot}4958 - 0{\cdot}2160 \text{ Log } r_s - 0{\cdot}1859 \text{ Log } K + 1{\cdot}2992 \text{ Log } \bar{Y}$$
$$(0{\cdot}0234) \qquad\quad (0{\cdot}2114) \qquad\quad (0{\cdot}0963)$$

The revision made the influence of wealth appear even more doubtful, although it showed stronger influences for both interest and income. A test was also made for the liquidity trap by computing partial elasticities of demand for income with respect to interest for various types of holders at varying ranges of interest; there was no significant increase of elasticity as interest fell.

The doubtful coefficient for the influence of wealth upon liquidity could arise from a strong association between wealth and income; wealth, on one view, is only capitalized property income. Meltzer[1] tested, for the period 1900–58, two estimates, one omitting K and the other omitting Y. (Both used the bond rate, r_b, the yield on twenty-year corporate bonds.) He obtained

$$\text{Log } L = -0{\cdot}79 \text{ Log } r_b + 1{\cdot}05 \text{ Log } Y + \text{constant}$$
$$\text{Log } L = -0{\cdot}90 \text{ Log } r_b + 1{\cdot}15 \text{ Log } K + \text{constant}$$

The statistical significance of the coefficient for K was found to be greater than that for Y and, as this finding confirmed a theoretical argument, Meltzer preferred the second type of equation. He, too, found no evidence for a liquidity trap, and showed that his results were little affected by using various definitions of money or wealth.

The most thorough test of liquidity functions is that recently made by Teigen,[2] who directly compares his own results with those of Bronfenbrenner and Mayer. Unlike them, and other investigators, he tried to estimate an equation for the supply of money, instead of taking this as given, so as to separate better supply from demand influences. He found, for the period 1924–1941, an interest-elasticity of demand of 0·0907 which was close

[1] *Journal of Political Economy*, 1963.
[2] *Econometrica*, 1964.

73

to theirs. But he found an income-elasticity of demand of 0·4432, higher than their estimate of 0·3440 and, unlike Meltzer, preferred to exclude wealth from the explanation instead of income.

For the later period, 1946–59, using quarterly data, he found an interest-elasticity of only 0·0168 and also a much lower income-elasticity of 0·1613. These decreases are puzzling, especially that of interest-elasticity; Teigen thinks it may be connected with the function of money becoming much more a means of payment and, owing to rapid growth of saving deposits and short-term bonds, much less a store of value. If so, it would mean that monetary policy has become less able to influence the American economy, either through changes in liquidity or through associated changes in rates of interest.

6.3 Conclusions

Economic exploration of liquidity functions is at about the same pioneering stage as that of investment functions. The one certain conclusion, so far, is that demand for liquidity is negatively or inversely related to interest rates, but interest rates do not appear to be very sensitive to changes in liquidity, at least in countries with highly organized capital markets where other financial intermediaries than banks provide various kinds of substitutes for money as a means of holding wealth in reasonably liquid form. Keynes's liquidity trap has not yet been proved a bogey, but it lacks really convincing statistical evidence. Theoretical arguments for it, moreover, are less than compelling. As Bronfenbrenner and Mayer have pointed out, although each individual may cease holding securities, exchanging them for money balances, at some low rate of interest, this rate will differ between individuals, and there is no reason for thinking that the demand for money holdings becomes infinitely elastic at any particular rate until the last bondholder has sold out. If, further, interest rates are falling rapidly, or bond prices rising, this may generate such new expectations of capital gains as to make people reduce their ideas of a 'normal' rate of interest.

It also seems clear that demand for liquidity is positively

74

related to income or wealth, or to some intermediate variable such as permanent income or previous holdings of liquid assets. Statistical estimation here is handicapped by the fact that these variables cannot all be independent. Recent evidence seems to favour that version of the permanent income hypothesis which points to the use of current income together with previous holdings of liquidity, but the issue is far from being settled.

One thing that has become apparent is that it is no longer sufficient, in either theoretical or econometric work, to take the supply of liquidity as given or exogenous. Such an assumption would be appropriate if there were a single authority issuing, or fully controlling the issue of money, and if money had no close substitutes either as a means of payment or as a store of value. Then it might be possible to explain prices or interest rates in terms of monetary changes in accordance with some equation such as

$$\frac{M}{P} = l_1 Y - l_2 r.$$

(If l_2 equals zero, or if r is determined in some other way we should have $P = \frac{1}{l_1} \frac{M}{Y}$, i.e. the simple quantity theory of money.) But no authority does have the power of fully controlling the issue of money or money substitutes, and our models should say something about what determines their supply.

Teigen's work has shown how important such extension is for the statistical estimation of influences upon liquidity demand itself. But the formulation, let alone the testing, of supply functions is still at a primitive stage. Following simple models of Meade and Modigliani, Teigen makes the supply of money, defined as currency plus demand deposits, depend upon the reserves of commercial banks, their lending rate and the central bank's discount rate. The definition of money may be regarded as too narrow, and the determinants relate only to that part of the supply which is under central banking control. Even then the determinants are over-simplified so that it is hardly surprising to find Teigen's estimate of the supply function was statistically inferior to his estimates of liquidity demand. It would seem necessary to relate supply also to competitive rates of interest offered by other financial intermediaries, and perhaps to distinguish, in the case of commercial banks, interest on securities from interest on loans. Work along such lines has been urged, and partly done, by Gurley and Shaw[1] but their results, and the questions they raise, are not discussed here because they are rather complex and, as yet, by no means convincing.

[1] See especially, *Money and the Theory of Finance*, (1960).

CHAPTER 7

Foreign Trade

7.1 Imports

Imports enter, both as final and as intermediate goods, into supplies of domestic consumption and investment, and often also into exports. Demands for imports, therefore, should depend upon much the same influences as those which determine consumption or investment. As imports are usually a large component of stocks they are especially likely to be influenced by investment in stocks.

Even in the United States, where foreign trade is relatively small, Bassie[1] found a strong connection between import demand and new investment in inventories. His equation, for the period 1922–56 was:

$$M_\theta = 47\cdot3 + 0\cdot533H_\theta + 2\cdot67V_\theta$$

where H denotes 'flow of goods to final users' or national output less personal services, government consumption, net foreign lending and one-half of building construction.

An influence from investment in stocks was also recognized by the Netherlands Central Planning Bureau,[2] as well as one from domestic demand. But it recognized another distinctive influence from the comparative prices of domestic and foreign goods, P and P_m; to the extent that imports are substitutes for domestic production we should expect that the demand for them is stimulated by a fall in their own prices or by a rise in prices of domestic substitutes. The Bureau's equation was:

$$M_\theta = 1\cdot60Y_\theta + 2\cdot34\left(\frac{V_\theta - V_{\theta-1}}{V_\theta}\right) - 0\cdot76\left(\frac{P_m}{P}\right)_\theta - 0\cdot53.$$
$$\quad(0\cdot14)\quad(0\cdot37)\qquad\qquad\quad(0\cdot16)$$

[1] *Economic Forecasting* (1958), p. 276.
[2] P. J. Verdoorn and C. J. van Eyck, op. cit., p. 20.

In this equation it is the growth rate of investment in stocks, not the level of such investment, which is taken to influence import demand.

A recent model for Japan[1] recognizes the influences of domestic demand and investment in stocks, but not that of relative prices. It gives two import functions, over semi-annual periods from 1953 to 1962, one for raw materials and fuels, M^1, and the other for remaining imports, M^2. They were estimated as:

$$M_\theta^1 = 19{\cdot}07 + 4{\cdot}5120 O_\theta + 0{\cdot}116 V_\theta$$
$$\phantom{M_\theta^1 = 19{\cdot}07 + {}} (0{\cdot}337) \quad (0{\cdot}015)$$

$$M_\theta^2 = -99{\cdot}6 + 0{\cdot}0625 I_\theta + 0{\cdot}0731 \, (Y^G - I)_\theta - 0{\cdot}952 z$$
$$\phantom{M_\theta^2 = -99{\cdot}6 + {}} (0{\cdot}0391) \quad (0{\cdot}0203) \phantom{ + 0{\cdot}0731} (0{\cdot}257)$$

where O denotes industrial output, Y^G the G.N.P. and z an allowance for seasonal variation.

In their model for the United States, Klein and Goldberger ignored stocks but combined the influence of domestic demand with that of relative prices in measuring income by its purchasing power over imports. They found

$$M_\theta = 2{\cdot}09 + 0{\cdot}009 \, Y_\theta \left(\frac{P}{P_m} \right)_\theta + 0{\cdot}24 M_{\theta-1}.$$
$$\phantom{M_\theta = 2{\cdot}09 + {}} (0{\cdot}006) \phantom{Y_\theta \left(\frac{P}{P_m} \right)_\theta} (0{\cdot}12)$$

This equation resembles their consumption function by allowing an influence from the previous value of the dependent variable. But neither of the parameters are well estimated.

One difficulty which often confronts investigators of import demand is the curb imposed by controls over imports or exchange in countries having trouble with the balance of payments. Klein[2] met this difficulty in his annual prototype model for the United Kingdom, 1946–56, by introducing, as an explanatory variable, the gold and dollar reserves which have an obvious, if

[1] Economic Planning Agency: *Econometric Models for Medium-term Economic Plan, 1964–1968*, (1965), pp. 25–26.

[2] Klein, Ball, Hazelwood and Vandome, *An Econometric Model of the United Kingdom* (1961).

not very exact, connection with the severity or restriction. The equation was

$$M_\theta = 7 \cdot 29 + 0 \cdot 92 O_\theta - 0 \cdot 046 \left(\frac{P_m}{P} \right) + 0 \cdot 044 R_\theta$$

where O is again an index of industrial output and R the ratio of reserves at the beginning of the year to imports two years previously.

In their corresponding quarterly model for the United Kingdom, Klein and his collaborators grouped imports into three classes – food, basic materials and other imports. Apart from allowances for seasonal factors, the influences were much the same as in the annual model. Food imports depended on previous food consumption and upon the reserves, as did other imports. The equation for imports of materials, however, also recognized an influence from investment in stocks as it had a term for the ratio of stocks to previous imports. (The equation for other imports had a term for the previous prices of metal imports.)

These examples, of course, are only a small selection from many empirical import functions. They illustrate, nevertheless, the main influences recognized in such functions, which might be summed up by a formal expression,

$$M = f(C, V, F, \frac{P}{P_m}, M_{-1}, R).$$

So far as it goes, this accords with general economic theory, although as a typically crude macro-version.

7.2 Exports
Since exports from one country are part of the imports entering other countries they ought to depend upon similar influences there; e.g. foreign demand levels, foreign import restrictions and relative prices. But, as exports further depend upon competition from other suppliers to world markets, the influence of such competition has also to be recognized.

The equation used by the Netherlands Central Planning Bureau was

$$X_\theta = 1\cdot10X^c_{\theta-1} - 0\cdot77\,(P_x - P^c_x)_{\theta-1} + 2.38$$
$$(0\cdot06) \qquad (0\cdot26)$$

where X^c denoted the volume of competitive exports and P^c_x their price. It is obvious from the positive influence of P^c_x on X that Dutch exports are substitutes for other countries' exports in world markets. But X^c, a weighted average of exports from the United States, the United Kingdom, Western Germany, France, Belgium-Luxemburg and Denmark, also has a positive sign, indicating a complementary rather than a competitive relation. It is, however, explained that 'after some experimentation the best yardstick for effective export demand was found in the total exports of those countries that are in close competition with the Netherlands in foreign markets'. The above equation refers to the quantity of Dutch exports, the value of which also depends upon Dutch export prices. These prices were explained by the equation (in which l denotes unit labour cost),

$$P_x = 1\cdot58X^c + 0\cdot382l + 0\cdot514P_m - 1\cdot51$$

and, if this is substituted into the preceding equation, we have

$$X_\theta = 3\cdot54 - 0\cdot12X^c_{\theta-1} - \cdot77P^c_{x\cdot\theta-1} - \cdot40P_{m\cdot\theta-1} - \cdot29l_{\theta-1}$$

The influence of import prices here reflects the import content of Dutch exports.

The Japanese model has a similar export equation, viz.

$$\text{Log } X_\theta = 2\cdot786 + 1\cdot774 \text{ Log } X^w_\theta - 1\cdot524 \text{ Log }\left(\frac{P_\theta}{P^w}\right)_\theta$$
$$(0\cdot121) \qquad\qquad (0\cdot258)$$

X^w denoting exports of the non-Communist world and P^w the export price index of manufactures for eleven leading industrial countries. Here, too, X^w indicates world demand conditions for Japanese exports and P^w the price competition of rival suppliers in world markets.

Klein and his collaborators on the model for the United Kingdom give two export functions, one for food, X_f, and the other for metals and engineering products, X_e. The first equation, omitting terms for seasonal influences, was

$$X_{f.\theta} = 35 \cdot 21 + \underset{(0 \cdot 12)}{0 \cdot 71} \; O^w_{f.\theta-3} + \underset{(0 \cdot 54)}{0 \cdot 95} \left(\frac{P^w_f}{P_f}\right)_{\theta-3}$$

where O^w_f is an index of world food output, P^w_f an index of world food prices and P_f an index of prices for British food goods. The second equation was

$$X_{e.\theta} = 18 \cdot 31 + \underset{(0 \cdot 07)}{0 \cdot 94} \; O^w_{e.\theta-1}$$

where O^w_e is an index of world production of similar products; an attempt was made to include relative prices but the estimate of the corresponding parameter proved quite unsatisfactory.

An interesting feature of this United Kingdom model was the attempt to estimate separate export functions for total British exports to various areas – the dollar area, O.E.E.C. countries, the independent sterling area and the dependent sterling area. In these empirical functions demand conditions in the importing area, as indicated by production, employment or exports, were the dominant influence. Exports to the dollar area also depended upon the ratio of industrial prices there to those of British exports. Both parts of the sterling area, which also made use of import controls, showed another influence from previous holdings of sterling balances. Total export functions, accordingly, represent the same kind of determinants as appeared in corresponding equations for British imports.

In this chapter we have been concerned only with the narrow problems of empirical demand functions for imports and exports. There are, of course, much wider problems of foreign trade, even at the macro-level, but it seems best to defer their discussion until Chapter 16 which will consider them in the light of economic policy.

CHAPTER 8

Labour

8.1 Production Functions and Perfect Competition

Demand for labour[1], L, as for other factors, is derived from that for output by means of a production function which relates the supply of output to required supplies of primary factors. Employment, obviously enough, depends on output, but does it not also depend upon the price of labour, or rather upon the price of labour relative to other factor prices? The theory that entrepreneurs seek to maximize profits, subject to the constraints imposed by a production function, shows that it does.

Profit is revenue less cost, or

$$R = pY - (wL + rK).$$

Under conditions of perfect competition all prices are taken as given by individual entrepreneurs so that, given such competition, the necessary conditions for maximum profit are

$$\frac{\partial R}{\partial L} = 0 = p\frac{\partial Y}{\partial L} - w$$

$$\frac{\partial R}{\partial K} = 0 = p\frac{\partial Y}{\partial K} - r.$$

The real wage rate, then, is equal to the marginal product of labour, and the real rent of capital to its marginal product; i.e.

$$\frac{w}{p} = \frac{\partial Y}{\partial L}, \quad \frac{r}{p} = \frac{\partial Y}{\partial K}.$$

[1] I hope no confusion arises from using here the same symbol as was previously used for liquidity.

82

These marginal products have now to be derived from a production function. The simplest one has the *linear* form

$$Y = A + lL + kK$$

giving marginal products as

$$\frac{\partial Y}{\partial L} = \frac{w}{p} = l, \quad \frac{\partial Y}{\partial K} = \frac{r}{p} = k.$$

The demand for labour is thus

$$L = \frac{p}{w}(Y - A) - \frac{r}{w}K$$

varying in the same way as demand for output and in the opposite way to factor prices.

It is natural for a rise in the wage-rate to damp the demand for labour. But why should this demand also be reduced by a rise in the price of capital? Our odd result is a consequence of the linear production function which does not allow for any change in the marginal product of a factor as more or less of it is employed. The ratio of the marginal products of two factors, when output is held constant, gives their marginal rate of substitution, here

$$\frac{dL}{dK} = \frac{\partial Y}{\partial K} \Big/ \frac{\partial Y}{\partial L} = \frac{k}{l},$$

and the elasticity of substitution between two factors is the relative change in their proportions to that in their marginal rate of substitution here, as the marginal rate of substitution is constant,

$$\sigma = \frac{d \log \left(\dfrac{L}{K} \right)}{d \log \left(\dfrac{dL}{dK} \right)} = \infty$$

so that a linear production function takes labour and capital as perfect substitutes!

The difficulty of assuming constant marginal products is

83

removed by the famous Cobb-Douglas production function, which is *linear-logarithmic* in form, i.e.

$$Y = AL^l K^k \text{ or Log } Y = \text{Log } A + l \text{ Log } L + k \text{ Log } K$$
$$l + k = 1$$

This gives marginal products as

$$\frac{\partial Y}{\partial L} = lAL^{l-1}K^k = \frac{lAL^l K^k}{L} = l\frac{Y}{L} = \frac{w}{p}$$

$$\frac{\partial Y}{\partial K} = kAL^l K^{k-1} = \frac{kAL^l K^k}{K} = k\frac{Y}{K} = \frac{r}{p}$$

and so demand for labour as

$$L = l\left(\frac{p}{w}\right) Y = l\left(\frac{p}{w}\right)\frac{K}{k}\left(\frac{r}{p}\right) = \left(\frac{lr}{kw}\right)K$$

Demand for labour is now seen as increasing if the demand for output or for capital increases, if the real price of capital rises, or if the real price of labour falls. In technical terms, capital is here a substitute for labour with a constant level of output, but may be a complement to labour with a rising level of output.

This is satisfactory so far as it goes. But the Cobb-Douglas function has the peculiarity of making the elasticity of substitution unity, whereas theory suggests it may have any positive value, however large. For here

$$\sigma = \frac{d \text{ Log }\left(\frac{L}{K}\right)}{d \text{ Log }\left(\frac{kL}{lK}\right)} = \frac{d \text{ Log }\left(\frac{L}{K}\right)}{d \text{ Log }\left(\frac{k}{l}\right) + d \text{ Log }\left(\frac{L}{K}\right)} = 1.$$

The restriction is removed by a new function which has been advanced by Arrow, Chenery, Minhas and Solow.[1] It is horribly called the *homohypallagic* function and has the form

$$Y = \gamma\left[lL^{-\rho} + kK^{-\rho}\right]^{-\frac{1}{\rho}}, \qquad l + k = 1$$

[1] *Review of Economics and Statistics*, 1961.

It follows that

$$dY = Z\left[-\rho lL^{-(\rho+1)}\,dL - \rho kK^{-(\rho+1)}\,dK\right]$$

if we put

$$Z = -\frac{\gamma}{\rho}\left[lL^{-\rho} + kK^{-\rho}\right]^{-\left(\frac{1}{\rho}+1\right)}$$

Hence the marginal rate of substitution becomes

$$\frac{\partial Y}{\partial K}\bigg/\frac{\partial Y}{\partial L} = \frac{\rho kK^{-(\rho+1)}}{\rho lL^{-(\rho+1)}} = \frac{k}{l}\left(\frac{L}{K}\right)^{\rho+1}$$

The elasticity of the substitution is then

$$\sigma = \frac{d\,\mathrm{Log}\left(\dfrac{L}{K}\right)}{d\,\mathrm{Log}\left[\dfrac{k}{l}\left(\dfrac{L}{K}\right)^{\rho+1}\right]} = \frac{d\,\mathrm{Log}\left(\dfrac{L}{K}\right)}{(\rho+1)\,d\,\mathrm{Log}\left(\dfrac{L}{K}\right)} = \frac{1}{1+\rho}$$

and is evidently not necessarily unity. The marginal rate of substitution can now be written as

$$\frac{k}{l}\left(\frac{L}{K}\right)^{\frac{1}{\sigma}} = \frac{r}{w},$$

Using this result we obtain the demand for labour as

$$L = \left(\frac{lr}{kw}\right)^{\sigma} K$$

which is clearly a generalization of the previous Cobb-Douglas result.

But we can also express demand for labour in terms of output. The function may be written as

$$\left(\frac{1}{\gamma}Y\right)^{-\rho} = lL^{-\rho} + kK^{-\rho}$$

and, since

$$K = \left(\frac{lr}{kw}\right)^{-\sigma} \cdot L$$

$$\rho = \frac{1-\sigma}{\sigma}$$

we obtain

$$\left(\frac{1}{\gamma}Y\right)^{-\rho} = L^{-\rho}\left[l + k\left(\frac{lr}{kw}\right)^{1-\sigma}\right]$$

and

$$L = \frac{1}{\gamma}Y\left[l + k\left(\frac{lr}{kw}\right)^{1-\sigma}\right]^{\frac{\sigma}{1-\sigma}}.$$

Demand for labour thus increases with output, and with the price of capital, but decreases with the price of labour. Its response, moreover, to changes in factor prices is greater if the elasticity of substitution is large than if the elasticity is small. The homohypallagic function thus accords well with theory.

8.2 Empirical Results
Klein and Goldberger had little success in finding a statistical production function for the United States. Trying a simple linear relation they found

$$Y_\theta = 31 \cdot 98 + 2 \cdot 31 L_\theta + 0 \cdot 08 K_\theta + 1 \cdot 90 \ (\theta - 1929).$$
$$(0 \cdot 18) \quad (0 \cdot 06) \quad (0 \cdot 15)$$

The parameter for capital is positive but very small and unreliable. They found a better equation for the wage bill (demand for labour multiplied by the wage-rate)

$$W_\theta = -2 \cdot 70 + 0 \cdot 35 Y_\theta + 0 \cdot 14 Y_{\theta-1} + 0 \cdot 16 \ (\theta - 1929)$$
$$(0 \cdot 04) \quad (0 \cdot 03) \quad (0 \cdot 08)$$

but one which ignores relative factor prices.

The Netherlands Central Planning Bureau has introduced relative commodity prices into an empirical production function, but not relative factor prices. This function is

$$L_\theta = 0.61\,Y_\theta + 0.52 \left(\frac{R}{Y}\right)_\theta + 0.11 \left(\frac{P_m}{P}\right)_\theta$$
$$(0.07)\quad (0.13)\qquad (0.03)$$
$$+ \begin{bmatrix} 15.79\ \text{Log}\ R_{\theta-1} - 21.70\ \text{Log}\ L_{\theta-1} \\ (6.88)\qquad\qquad (6.58) \end{bmatrix} + 0.57.$$

$\dfrac{P_m}{P}$ denotes the ratio of import prices to local prices, and the bracketed expression comes from a particular hypothesis about entrepreneurial expectations – a version of the permanent income hypothesis.

In their quarterly model for the United Kingdom, Klein and his collaborators obtained the function

$$O_\theta = 58.71 + 0.94\ [(hL)_\theta + 0.60M_\theta] + 0.13\theta$$
$$(0.17)\qquad\qquad\qquad (0.19)$$

which makes industrial output depend upon total hours (h) of labour worked and also upon imports. They, too, ignored capital, and so relative factor prices.

Murray Brown[1] has fitted an equation, based on the homo-hypallagic function, for private, non-farm demand for labour to U.S. annual data. His result for the sub-period 1938–58 was

$$\text{Log}\ L = 0.8196 + 1.2456\ \text{Log}\ Y - 0.1873\ \text{Log}\theta.$$
$$\phantom{\text{Log}\ L = 0.8196 +}(0.1673)\qquad\qquad (0.0539)$$

The term for relative factor prices was omitted only because it proved statistically insignificant. It is disappointing that this attempt, founded on a sophisticated theoretical approach, proved hardly better than much cruder estimates.

Even less success has attended efforts to estimate a supply function for labour, although Tintner[2] made valiant efforts to find one for the United Kingdom. Most empirical work seems to have become directed to 'wage-adjustment equations', relating wage changes to change in the demand for labour, as indicated by unemployment or similar statistics. These, however, do not throw direct light upon demand for labour but rather upon prices of labour and goods. We postpone their consideration, accordingly, to our discussion of inflation.

[1] *On the Theory and Measurement of Technological Change* (1960), p. 175.
[2] *Econometrica* (1952), p. 143.

87

CHAPTER 9

Some Practical Models

After this discussion of empirical behaviour relations it will be as well to gain some idea about the way they fit together in a model describing a whole economy. Most empirical models, however, are too complicated for any brief explanation and those described here have been chosen because of their simplicity rather than for their accuracy or up-to-dateness.

9.1 A Simple Forecasting Model for the United States

Ta-Chung Liu has offered a simple forecasting model for the United States.[1] It fits the data quite well for the period 1930–52, and surprisingly well for the war years when ordinary economic relations were much disturbed.

There are only four endogenous variables in the model, and another four predetermined variables:

Y = gross national product, t^* = taxes per unit of Y,
$Y^{(d)}$ = disposable personal income, T^* = government transfers,
C = personal consumption, D^* = defence expenditures,
F = private fixed capital A^* = other expenditure.
      formation,

D^* like A^* is autonomous, but has a separate role as an index of the intensity of official measures to restrain private spending during the period of war inflation.

The structural equations comprise an income identity, a technical relation between disposable income and GNP, a consumption function, an investment function and a liquidity function.

$$(1.1) \qquad\qquad Y = C + I + A^*$$

[1] *I.M.F. Staff Papers*, 1954–55.

(1.2) $Y^{(d)} = 0.664\,(Y+T^*) - 0.699t^* + 19.038$
               (0.010)   (0.212)

(1.3) $C = 0.640\,Y^{(d)} + 0.342L - 0.0036D^* + 2.335$
               (0.087)   (0.096)   (0.0004)

(1.4) $I = 0.161\,Y + 0.031\,Y_{-1} - 0.0029D^* - 0.470t^* - 1.397$
         (0.038)   (0.038)   (0.0002)   (0.238)

(1.5) $L = 0.232\,Y + 0.409\,Y_{-1} + 1.493.$
                  (0.155)   (0.173)

From these equations he deduces

(1.6a) $Y = 0.51\,Y_{-1} - 0.19D^* + 3.00A^* + 1.27T^* - 2.57t^* + 40.087$

and similar equations can be obtained for C, I and L expressing each of them as a function of lagged or predetermined variables. Forecasts are obtained when values of these lagged or predetermined variables are inserted in equations such as (1.6a). When actual values for 1952 were thus inserted, a forecast was obtained giving Y as \$335.8 b. which was only 3.5 per cent below the actual value of Y in 1952, \$348.0 b.

For forecasting purposes it is possible to dispense with the knowledge obtained of structural coefficients by computing equations (1.2) to (1.5). These structural coefficients, in any case, do not seem likely to be very reliable because the behaviour relations are highly simplified; the consumption function has no lags, the investment function neglects the capital stock, and the liquidity function neglects interest, to mention only a few defects. But more elaborate behaviour relations would not necessarily involve more predetermined variables. Liu, therefore, estimated another forecasting equation by taking regressions of Y (C, I and L) upon the predetermined variables; in this way he directly estimates the influence of the whole set of predetermined variables upon an endogenous variable, instead of deducing this influence from estimates of the structural equations. He obtained

(1.6b) $Y = 0.42\,Y_{-1} - 0.011D^* + 2.22A^* + 4.25T^* - 2.45t^* + 46.89.$
          (0.10)   (0.002)   (0.28)   (1.10)   (1.08)

89

It will be seen that coefficients differ between (1·6a) and(1.6b). The forecast for 1952 GNP given by (1.6b) was \$344·9 b. and because this involved an error of only 0·9 per cent, as against one of 3·5 per cent for (1.6a), the result tells in favour of the second procedure.

Liu goes on to compare a forecasting model very similar to (1.6b) (differing only by recalculation to include 1952 data), with two 'naive' models, the first of which (I) assumes Y has the same value as in the previous year, and the second (II) that Y increases by the same amount as in the previous year. Each naive model did better than the forecast model in only 5 out of the 24 years, and over the whole period mean-square errors were 364·51 for I, 214·12 for II and 33·89 for the equation. As he says, it is 'a far more reliable forecasting device than either of the two naive models'.

9.2 A Dutch Planning Model

The 1955 model that was used by the Netherlands Central Planning Bureau[1] for policy purposes is much more elaborate, having 24 endogenous and 14 predetermined variables. It has, however, only five behaviour equations so that a simplified version of it can be given here, ignoring mainly technical problems of measurement.

The main purpose of the model is to explain business activity and, in effect, it has 9 equations for this purpose.

(1) $\quad Y + M = C + G^* + F + V^* + X$

(2) $\quad N = 0 \cdot 40 \, (Y + M - V^*)$

(3) $\quad W = N w^*$

(4) $\quad R = Y - W - T_i{}^*$

(5) $\quad C = 0 \cdot 85 \, (W + W^* - T_w{}^*) + 0 \cdot 40 \, (R - T_r{}^*)$

(6) $\quad F = 0 \cdot 25 \, (Y + M - V^*) - 0 \cdot 10 \, F_{-1}$

---

[1] Descriptions of this model are given in H. Theil, *Economic Forecasts and Economic Policy* (1958), pp. 52–56 and Central Planning Bureau, *Scope and Methods of the Central Planning Bureau* (1956). But the author has also used data obtained during a visit to the Bureau in 1958. Since then a somewhat more elaborate model has been used; cp *Central Planning Bureau, Monograph No. 10, Forecasts and Realization* (1965).

$$(7) \qquad X = X^* - 2 \cdot 00 \, (p_x - p_w{}^*)$$
$$(8) \qquad p_x = 0 \cdot 18_w{}^* + 0 \cdot 16 p_m{}^* + 0 \cdot 50 p_w$$
$$(9) \qquad M = 0 \cdot 38 C + 0 \cdot 39 G^* + 0 \cdot 71 F + 0 \cdot 79 V^* + 0 \cdot 63 X.$$

The variables are all to be understood here as relating to business output, not to national output. Thus G denotes government purchases from business and W wages paid by business, W^* denoting other wage payments. As before T represents net transfers to the state and p_w competitive world prices; exogenous variables, or those independently forecast such as V, p_m and p_w, are starred.

The model thus begins with independent forecasts of government purchases from business (G^*), the prospective change in business inventories (V^*), import prices (p_m^*) and competitive export prices (p_w^*), net transfers from business (T_x^*), and profit recipients (T_r^*) to the state, government wage payments (W^*) and the average wage rate (w^*). This wage rate, in accordance with Dutch law, was supposed to be fixed by official tribunals as an actual, not merely a minimum, wage rate.

The model would then forecast simultaneously business output (Y), employment (N), profits (R), fixed investment (F), exports (X), and imports (M). Employment depends here upon a simple production function (2) which relates short-term changes in output (gross of imports!) only to labour. Consumption output depends not only upon private income but also upon its division between wage-earners and others. Fixed investment is explained by a flexible accelerator or capacity principle. Exports depend upon expected demands abroad for the goods sold there by the Netherlands (X^*) and upon the relation of Dutch export prices to those of its rivals; Dutch export prices, in turn, depend on the level at which wages are fixed, upon import prices (as exports have a substantial import content) and upon competitive world prices (as these affect profit margins in export costing). Imports depend, not only on output, but also upon its division between the various major components of demand.

The model was recomputed each year as additional data became available, and the coefficients given above were found for data up to 1954. If forecasts gave unacceptable results, in the policy year under consideration, changes would be suggested to the government for reaching better results. The value of such advice, of course, depends upon the model's reliability. Tests were made, for 1955, 1956 and 1957, of the model against three naive forecasting procedures, viz.

   I. a no change forecast
  II. an equal change forecast
 III. forecasts based on the auto-correlation of the endogenous variable, i.e. projecting its level on the basis of its own previous levels

The standardized root-mean-square errors over all forecast variables are shown below.

	1955 Model	Model I	Model II	Model III
1955	0·48	1·37	0·45	0·91
1956	0·85	1·49	0·51	1·05
1957	0·29	0·65	1·33	0·53
1955–57	0·57	1·23	0·86	0·86

The planning model definitely gave better forecast results. Another test was the number of turning points correctly predicted, and here results were less satisfactory. The 1955 model correctly predicted, over the period 1923–38 and 1949–57, only 39 out of a total of 89 actual turning points; it gave no prediction in 36 cases, 9 opposite predictions and 36 predictions that were not realized.

But forecasts are only one purpose of the planning model. The policy purpose is to estimate the effects of changes in taxes or government expenditures upon the endogenous variables, more especially upon income, employment, prices, exports and imports. Below is an abbreviated table, based on the 1955 model, showing how the effect of various policy measures upon key variables may be read off.

Change in	$\Delta G =$ Fl. 100m.	$\Delta T_i =$ Fl. 100m.	$\Delta T_r =$ Fl. 100m.	$\Delta T_w =$ Fl. 100m.	$\Delta w =$ 1 p.c.
$Y + M$ (Fl.m.)	131	−140	−55	−111	0–23
C "	19	−127	−50	−101	−19
F "	12	−13	−5	−10	−2
X-M "	−55	61	24	48	−1
M "	55	−61	−24	−48	19
R "	49	−58	−19	−40	−25
X "	...	...	...	...	−40
L "	0·107	−0·111	−0·043	−0·088	−0·010
P_x "	...	...	...	...	0·180

It is also of interest to note the theoretical effects of a 10 per cent devaluation of the guilder. These would be, on the basis of the 1955 model.

$$\Delta X = + Fl\, 1{,}200m \text{ and } \Delta M = - Fl\, 1{,}812m.$$

9.3 A Recent Model for New Zealand

Bergstrom and Brownlie[1] have briefly reported an experimental model that they fitted to annual New Zealand data for the period 1949–64. They reached it from a much larger model by successive elimination of variables or equations which gave wrong signs or large sampling errors.

The model thus reached has two definitional relations, which may be written as

(1) $$Y = C + G + F + V + X - M$$
(2) $$E = C + G + F$$

and three behaviour relations described as a domestic expenditure function,

(3) $$E = -81·79 + 0·546 \, (Y + Y_{-1})$$
$$(0·033)$$

a production decision equation,

[1] *Economic Record*, 1965 and 1967.

(4) $\quad Y = -118{\cdot}27 + 0{\cdot}621\ [(Y-V)+(Y-V)_{-1}] - 0{\cdot}505K^v{}_{-1}$
$\qquad\qquad (0{\cdot}104) \qquad\qquad\qquad\qquad (0{\cdot}381)$

and an import function,

(5) $\quad M = -9{\cdot}78P^* + 0{\cdot}228\,Y_{-1}\left(\dfrac{P^*}{P^*_{-1}}\right) + 0{\cdot}968A_{-1}\left(\dfrac{P^*}{P_{-1}}\right)$
$\qquad\qquad (0{\cdot}017) \qquad\qquad\quad (0{\cdot}221)$

where P^* is the exogenous ratio of import prices to prices of consumers' goods and A is the annual average of net overseas assets. K^v is end-year level of stocks.

Equation (3) is interesting as making government expenditure depend in the same simple way upon income as does private expenditure, and so does not distinguish between government expenditure on consumption and fixed investment. There is, however, a hint of a capacity principle in equation (4) which could be interpreted as saying that investment in inventories rises with the level of output but falls with previous investment in inventories or with the previous stock. Equation (5) succeeds in explaining imports notwithstanding extensive controls, presumably because the intensity of such controls varies fairly systematically with the previous level of external reserves.

Imports can be directly forecast from (5) once an independent estimate or guess has been made for P^* Forecasts for the other dependent variables are obtained by rearranging the equations so that each dependent variable is expressed as a function of lagged or exogenous variables; viz.

$$Y = 0{\cdot}30\,Y_{-1}+0{\cdot}94(E-M)_{-1}-0{\cdot}76K^v{}_{-1}-0{\cdot}91A_{-1}+c_1X$$
$$(E-M)= 0{\cdot}48\,Y_{-1}+0{\cdot}52(E-M)_{-1}-0{\cdot}42K^v{}_{-1}-1{\cdot}47A_{-1}+c_2X$$
$$K^v = -0{\cdot}18\,Y_{-1}+0{\cdot}42(E-M)_{-1}+0{\cdot}66K^v{}_{-1}+0{\cdot}56A_{-1}+c_3X$$
$$A = -0{\cdot}23\,Y_{-1}$$

The authors show that any disturbance from equilibrium 'will be followed by a damped three-year cycle about a trend away from equilibrium. This result may reflect that omission from expenditure functions of stabilizing influences such as liquidity, interest and capital, and indicates that the model's usefulness may be limited to short-term forecasting'.

94

The accuracy of its forecasts also depends upon the independent estimates of P and X. A later article gives results, for 1965 and 1966, of unconditional forecasts, which were based on estimates for P, X and A, and conditional forecasts, which later insert actual values of P, X and A in order to test errors arising solely from the model.

Million.

Variable	1965			1966		
	Unconditional	Conditional	Actual	Unconditional	Conditional	Actual
Y	1,363	1,362	1,356	1,468	1,455	1,417
K^v	1	10	33	42	36	51
M	337	337	335	361	348	373

The forecasts for Y are good but a little inferior to those made by a naive model in which Y is a function only of Y_{-1}. The forecasts for K^v were inaccurate, but then so may be the 'actual' figures for this residual. Surprisingly enough the model did well, and better than naive models, in forecasting imports.

Part Three
Interindustry Analysis

CHAPTER 10

Interindustry Accounting

10.1 Breaking-down the Production Account

In the social accounts, and in the macro-models based upon them, we had a division of national expenditure, or aggregate demand, into private consumption, current government spending, capital formation and exports. This division corresponded to the different income and expenditure accounts which are, in effect, a break-down of the consolidated national income and expenditure account. Its principle was derived from differences between types of transactors, e.g. persons and governments, and between types of transactions, e.g. consumption and capital formation.

We had, however, a single national production account which netted out all intermediate transactions, and so showed only final outputs to the spending sectors together with primary inputs of labour, capital services and imports. Our macro-models thus treated output, or aggregate supply, employment, capital, prices and imports as single aggregates. This procedure is good enough for the purposes our models are designed to serve, but distinct advantages can be gained by breaking down the national production account into a number of different types of output, just as the national expenditure account is broken down into a number of different types of final demand.

The basis for such disaggregation is the classification of an economy's industries into a number of distinct *productive sectors*. For each sector we prepare a separate production account, similar to Table 1.1 but differing from it in that we now include intermediate outputs sold by one productive sector to another, as well as the final outputs sold to various income accounts. If that is done, we obtain a view of the inter-connections between productive sectors, as well as of their separate contributions to final demands and of their separate uses of primary inputs of labour, capital services and imports. Table 10.1 below illustrates a very simple breakdown of the national production account (p. 5) into the three broad productive sectors of primary, secondary and tertiary industry.

This division has long been used in Australia and New Zealand, and become familiar to other countries through the writings of A. G. B. Fisher and Colin Clark. Primary industry, Clark writes, includes agricultural and pastoral production, fishing, forestry and hunting.

Mining is more properly included with secondary production, covering manufacture, building construction and public works, gas and electricity supply. Tertiary production is defined by the difference, consisting of all other activities, the principal of which are distribution, transport, public administration, domestic service and all other activities producing a non-material output.[1]

Table 10.1 Matrix of Production Accounts (Input-Output)

Sales (outputs)	1	2	3	A	4	5	6	7	B	C
1. Primary industry	69	136	–	205	25	–	10	60	95	300
2. Secondary industry	51	612	237	900	475	40	105	180	800	1,700
3. Tertiary industry	30	255	110	395	300	150	135	20	605	1,000
4. Factor payments:										
a) wages	40	340	370	–	–	–	–	–	–	750
b) profits	90	40	120	–	–	–	–	–	–	250
5. Net expenditure taxes	6	85	39	–	–	–	–	–	–	130
6. Capital consumption	8	79	38	–	–	–	–	–	–	125
7. Imports, etc.	6	153	86	–	–	–	–	–	–	245
Total purchases	300	1,700	1,000	–	800	190	250	260	–	–

Key to column headings (horizontal)

1	Primary industry	5	Government income account
2	Secondary industry	6	National capital account
3	Tertiary industry	7	Exports, etc.
A	Total intermediate sales	B	Total final sales
4	Personal income account	C	Total sales

[1] C. G. Clark, *The Conditions of Economic Progress*, (1940), p. 182.

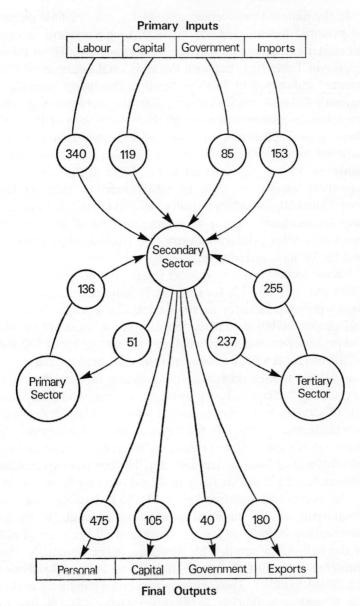

Figure 10.1 Inputs and Outputs of the Secondary Sector
(from Table 10.1)

In the national production account net sales of final output to personal income account are 800, to government income account 190 and to national capital account 250. These totals appear in Table 10.1, but with the additional information that primary industry sold 25 to personal consumption, secondary industry 475 and tertiary industry 300; the corresponding contributions to government consumption were 0, 40 and 150, and those to capital formation 10, 105 and 135. But, whereas in the national production account it was necessary to show only a figure of 15 for net external sales, Table 10.1, must show separately exports as 260, to which primary industry has contributed 60, secondary industry 180 and tertiary industry 20. Imports, similarly, appear as a separate item of 245, broken down into 6 for primary industry, 153 for secondary industry and 86 for tertiary industry.

Factor incomes in the national production account came to 1,000, now split into 750 for wages and 250 for profits. Table 10.1 shows primary industry as responsible for a wage-bill of 40 and profits of 90; secondary industry for a wage-bill of 340 and profits of 40, and tertiary industry for a wage-bill of 370 and profits of 120. It will be obvious that we have here treated wages paid by the household sector for domestic service, etc., as a payment by tertiary industry against a corresponding imputed sale of services by tertiary industry to households. Net expenditure taxes, shown as 130 in the national production account are broken down into 6 from primary industry, 85 from secondary industry and 39 from tertiary industry. The capital consumption allowances of 125 are similarly broken down into 8, 79 and 38.

The north-west quadrant of Table 10.1, however, has no counterpart in the national production account. It shows intermediate outputs or inputs, which had all been netted out of the national account. This quadrant is the essentially new feature of Table 10.1, showing as it does how industrial activities are linked together. Thus, although secondary industry makes the biggest contribution to final demands (800), it has to purchase materials of 136 from primary industry in order to do that, and 255 from tertiary industry, as well as having intra-sector purchases of intermediate goods amounting to 612. Of, if we read the table across instead of down, we see that tertiary industries derive 3 per cent of their total sales from primary industry, 25·5 per cent from secondary industry, 11 per cent from other tertiary industries and 60·5 per cent from final demands.

The immediate advantages of this breakdown of the national production account may be briefly listed.

(i) It shows the total output, of intermediate as well as of final goods, for each productive sector.

(ii) It shows the contribution each productive sector makes directly to final demand, as well as indirect contributions through sales of intermediate outputs to other sectors.

(iii) It shows, reading downwards, the cost structure of each productive sector, relating both to intermediate inputs and to final inputs.

(iv) It shows the demands made by each productive sector for labour and entrepreneurial services, for the services of capital equipment (in so far as these are reflected by depreciation allowances), and for imports, as well as the contributions levied for net expenditure taxes.

(v) Like all matrix presentations, it shows clearly the inter-connections between one productive sector and others, as well as those between producing sectors and spending sectors.

10.2 Problems of Classification

It will be shown, in the next chapter, that just as we can develop macro-models in order to forecast or control magnitudes appearing in the social accounts, so we can develop an input-output model to explain allocation of intermediate and primary inputs between productive sectors. This kind of model, however, is possible only if our classification of productive sectors meets a number of theoretical requirements. These requirements relate to the need for a single production function for each sector, and such a function can apply well only if outputs are reasonably homogeneous.

Ideally, the requirement of homogeneous sector outputs would mean a very fine classification of industries and, in practice, it is impossible to obtain sufficiently detailed information; even if this difficulty could be overcome the resulting table might well be too complicated to handle. The largest transaction matrices yet constructed is for 450 sectors, made by the U.S. Bureau of Labour in 1951, but most studies have ranged from 12 sectors in the New Zealand study of 1957 to 182 in the Japanese study of 1955.

The main practical difficulty about industrial classification is that statistics are collected from *establishments* which often produce, besides a major output, minor outputs such as joint products or by-products. In the Japanese study a serious attempt was made to make the classification of establishments into industries conform to theoretical requirements. Each establishment was assigned to an industry according to the major output it produced, but minor products were separated off and assigned, together with an appropriate imputation of inputs, to industries for which they were the major products. This commodity classification of industries is undoubtedly the correct approach but there is, of course, a serious difficulty in allocating separate inputs to each joint product.

The U.S. study made a practical compromise in order to avoid this difficulty. Each enterprise was assigned to an industry according to the major output which it produced. But minor outputs were treated both as part of its total output and as intermediate inputs of the industries for which they were major outputs by the device of dummy sales of minor products to these industries. Each output-row of the transactions matrix thus included all of the major output, in conformity to the commodity principle of industrial classification, but it also contained, as intermediate outputs, minor products of the establishments concerned. In most studies, however, the still more primitive practice is followed of lumping together, in value totals, minor products together with the industry's major product.

The next problem that arises is how to *value transactions*.

Theoretical requirements point to an f.o.b., as against a c.i.f., valuation, i.e. the valuation boundary is the selling sector so that the buying sector is charged with all distributive or transport costs. The transport and trading sectors have thus to be treated as agents for the buying sector, except when they purchase goods on their own capital accounts, and regarded as producing only the value of the services they render, as measured by their gross margins. This principle applies, in particular, to the external sector, goods sold to the rest of the world being valued at f.o.b. and goods purchased from it at c.i.f. Inward freight earnings, however, by resident transport concerns, should be treated as a credit from the external sector to the transport sector and, if imports involve domestic distributors, there has to be a similar transfer to the distribution sector.

Imports raise further problems. Some imports are competitive with domestic outputs, and others are complementary to them. Complementary imports, clearly enough, should be treated as an input of the sector which buys them. But this procedure, if followed for competitive imports, would obscure the dependence of industries upon a particular type of input supplied both from local and external sources. Chenery and Clark,[1] therefore, recommend treating competitive imports as inputs of the corresponding domestic outputs, and then allocating them, together with the domestic outputs, as sales to the sectors which use them. Stone and Croft-Murray,[2] make a similar recommendation, but suggest that competitive imports, instead of appearing as purchases of the domestic competitor, should be treated as negative exports by that competitor.

The final question considered here relates to outputs and inputs of consuming sectors. Table 10.1, following both Chenery and Stone, assigns to a service sector the 'outputs' of the household and government sectors, i.e. grower-consumed produce, net owner-rentals, domestic service and the value of work done

[1] H. B. Chenery and P. G. Clark, *Interindustry Economics*, (1959), p. 142.
[2] R. Stone and G. Croft-Murray, *Social Accounting and Economic Models*, (1959), p. 39.

Table 10.2 Input-Output Transactions, 1954-5 (£ million)

Source: N.Z. Department of Statistics, Report on the Interindustry Study of the N.Z. Economy in 1954-5

Output \ Input	Industrial sectors												Final demand					Total output
	1	2	3	4	5	6	7	8	9	10	11	12	13	14	15	16	17	
Industrial sectors																		
1 Farming	68·6	0·1	–	–	136·7	28·5	–	–	–	0·1	0·3	2·2	22·8	1·4	65·5	2·4	1·6	330·2
2 Forestry and logging	1·0	–	–	0·1	–	7·1	–	–	–	–	–	–	0·5	0·4	–	–	–	9·1
3 Hunting, fishing, etc.	–	–	–	–	0·1	0·2	–	–	–	–	–	0·3	1·1	1·3	1·2	–	–	4·2
4 Mining	–	–	–	–	0·9	3·0	4·1	1·1	1·2	–	0·2	0·7	1·7	0·2	0·5	–	–	13·6
5 Manufacturing primary produce processing	1·4	–	–	–	2·0	8·8	–	–	0·2	0·1	0·3	1·6	20·0	–	136·9	3·9	–	175·2
6 Manufacturing, other	28·8	0·9	0·5	1·9	1·8	83·1	47·0	2·2	14·8	12·2	3·8	16·0	218·6	4·5	18·8	10·9	32·5	498·3
7 Building and construction	1·0	–	–	0·2	0·4	4·4	–	0·3	1·8	0·5	5·1	1·8	5·4	15·8	0·1	3·7	117·1	157·6
8 Public utilities	1·2	–	–	0·1	0·7	3·6	0·2	0·3	0·3	1·8	0·5	2·3	11·3	2·1	–	–0·1	–	24·3
9 Transport and communication	7·9	0·2	0·1	1·3	5·3	11·8	7·6	0·4	5·7	22·6	2·9	4·1	25·3	4·6	17·6	–	5·0	122·4
10 Wholesale and retail trade	14·8	0·2	0·2	0·5	0·9	14·2	13·3	2·1	4·2	3·2	2·8	4·4	132·5	0·9	17·7	12·0	9·4	233·3
11 Banking and insurance	2·8	0·1	0·1	0·2	0·5	6·1	1·3	0·2	1·8	8·3	3·1	5·5	25·0	2·5	3·1	–	–	60·6
12 Services	4·9	–	–	0·2	0·6	5·5	0·7	0·2	1·3	9·8	4·3	20·1	68·6	52·1	3·0	–	–	171·3
Primary inputs																		
13 Net domestic output	172·7	6·3	2·9	8·0	20·6	160·3	60·8	14·7	69·8	138·8	31·3	94·8	29·8	21·8	–5·9	–	8·6	835·3
14 Rest of world – imports	10·9	0·7	0·3	0·5	2·8	114·3	20·0	1·6	9·8	4·9	1·3	9·4	65·8	15·9	1·8	6·6	32·8	299·4
15 Net indirect taxes	0·4	–	–	–	–	35·9	–	–0·4	2·1	21·9	0·5	4·9	2·1	–	–	–	–	67·4
16 Depreciation	13·8	0·6	0·1	0·6	1·9	11·5	2·6	1·6	9·4	9·1	4·2	3·2	3·8	–	–	–	0·1	62·5
Total input	330·2	9·1	4·2	13·6	175·2	498·3	157·6	24·3	122·4	233·3	60·6	171·3	634·3	123·5	260·3	39·4	207·1	3064·7

Key to column headings (horizontal)

1 Farming
2 Forestry and logging
3 Hunting, fishing, etc.
4 Mining
5 Manufacturing (primary produce processing)
6 Manufacturing, other
7 Building and construction
8 Public utilities
9 Transport and communication
10 Wholesale and retail trade
11 Banking and insurance
12 Services
13 Household purchases
14 Government purchases
15 Rest of world – exports
16 Stocks – net depreciation
17 Capital formation

by civil servants. It also treats as 'inputs' of such a sector, imports of finished goods, net expenditure taxes on consumer goods and depreciation on owner-occupied houses. But there is a variety of practice in this connection. The U.S. study of 1947 assigned all such inputs to the corresponding income accounts, while other studies have often followed a mixed procedure.

10.3   Examples of Transactions Matrices
Some examples of published transactions matrices will help to clarify the preceding discussion as well as to illustrate the importance of this type of representation. We begin with the old 1954–5 New Zealand study.

It should be explained that the row for net domestic output (13) combines wages and profits. Households and government output are assigned to corresponding final demand sectors, as are some imports, and some net expenditure taxes also appear as debits in the household income account. A major defect of this table was that sectors 2–4 are too small to warrant separate treatment in a 12-sector production account, but sector 6 is so big and complex that it should have been broken down into a number of separate manufacturing sectors; these defects were remedied in a later study.

As another example, we reproduce Richard Stone's rearrangement[1] of the table prepared by the U.K. Central Statistical Office.

As noted below, it differs from the American table in keeping both output and inputs of final demand sectors out of the south-west quadrant.

10.4   A Suggested Amalgamation
Richard Stone has made the valuable suggestion of combining both a matrix for the social accounts (p. 5) and an input-output matrix for production accounts into a single transactions matrix for all these accounts.[2] We should then obtain a most

---

[1] Op. cit., p. 33.
[2] R. Stone, *Input-Output and the Social Accounts*, Reprint No. 102 of Department of Applied Economics, University of Cambridge.

Table 10.3 Transactions Matrix for the United Kingdom, 1950

(£ million)

	1	2	3	4	5	6	7	8	9	10	11	12
1 Agriculture, forestry and fishing	0	0	3	0	28	563	14	0	0	1	0	490
2 Mining and quarrying	6	0	110	42	19	14	23	27	127	56	0	142
3 Chemicals and allied trades	77	24	0	104	30	59	52	59	7	88	0	415
4 Metals, engineering and vehicles	56	50	45	0	48	33	25	160	50	249	0	2368
5 Textiles, leather and clothing	10	5	15	41	0	13	92	3	1	27	0	1281
6 Food, drink and tobacco	116	0	10	0	1	0	0	0	0	15	0	2355
7 Other manufacturing	41	6	38	200	55	71	0	181	15	70	0	438
8 Building and contracting	30	21	8	22	15	8	4	0	2	73	0	1056
9 Gas, electricity and water	4	9	13	60	13	14	32	9	0	88	0	301
10 Other production and trade*	100	30	105	445	120	145	80	135	65	0	0	3851
11 Other industries†	0	0	0	0	0	0	0	0	0	0	0	2999
All other accounts consolidated	659	421	568	2170	1159	1577	793	665	276	4409	2999	0

Key to columns headings (horizontal)
1 Agriculture, forestry and fishing
2 Mining and quarrying
3 Chemicals and allied trades
4 Metals, engineering and vehicles
5 Textiles, leather and clothing
6 Food, drink and tobacco
7 Other manufacturing
8 Building and contracting
9 Gas, electricity and water
10 Other production and trade
11 Other industries
12 All other accounts consolidated

* Transport and communication distributive trades, insurance, banking and finance, and other services.
† Public administration and defence, public health and educational services, ownership of dwellings, domestic services to households, and services to private non-profit making bodies.

comprehensive view of the structure of the economy and of its complex interrelations. Table 10·4 opposite[1] illustrates this idea, although in rather a condensed form.

[1] Taken from Stone and Croft-Murray, *Social Accounting and Economic Models*, (1951), pp. 30–31.

(£ million)

	1	2	3	4	5	6	7	8	9	10	11	12	13	14	15	16
1 Agriculture, forestry and fishing	0	0	3	0	28	563	14	0	0	1	0	468	8	5	9	1,099
2 Mining and quarrying	6	0	110	42	19	14	23	27	127	56	0	99	4	–9	48	566
3 Chemicals and allied trades	77	24	0	104	30	59	52	59	7	88	0	215	51	–7	156	915
4 Metals, engineering and vehicles	56	50	45	0	48	33	25	160	50	249	0	260	217	809	1,082	3,084
5 Textiles, leather and clothing	10	5	15	41	0	13	92	3	1	27	0	828	3	–80	530	1,488
6 Food, drink and tobacco	116	6	10	0	1	0	0	0	0	15	0	2,170	16	40	129	2,497
7 Other manufacturing	41	21	38	200	55	71	0	181	15	70	0	198	95	–22	167	1,115
8 Building and contracting	30	8	8	22	15	8	4	0	2	73	0	243	150	661	2	1,239
9 Gas, electricity and water	4	9	13	60	13	14	32	9	0	88	0	230	28	39	4	543
10 Other production and trade*	100	30	105	445	120	145	80	135	65	0	0	2,892	293	123	543	5,076
11 Other industries†	0	0	0	0	0	0	0	0	0	0	0	1,745	1,206	–67	115	2,999
12 Business and households appropriation –																
Wages and Salaries	264	359	149	1,406	483	247	466	503	145	2,317	1,264	0	0	0	0	7,603
Profits, interest and rent	332	33	93	441	161	226	112	102	0	1,129	70	0	0	0	337	3,036
Public debt interest	0	0	0	0	0	0	0	0	0	0	0	0	551	0	0	551
Other current transfers	0	0	0	0	0	0	0	0	0	0	0	0	754	0	0	754
13 Government appropriation –																
Current transfers (taxes, less subsidies)	–44	3	70	11	11	678	11	7	23	313	504	2,251	0	0	0	3,838
14 Capital transactions –																
Depreciation	54	15	31	94	36	30	36	14	107	284	297	0	0	0	0	998
Saving	0	0	0	0	0	0	0	0	0	0	0	350	417	0	0	767
Capital transfers (net)	0	0	0	0	0	0	0	0	0	0	0	0	0	0	167	167
15 External –																
Goods and services	53	11	225	218	468	396	168	39	1	366	864	0	0	0	0	2,809
Current transfers (net)	0	0	0	0	0	0	0	0	0	0	0	–5	45	0	0	40
Lending (net)	0	0	0	0	0	0	0	0	0	0	0	0	0	440	0	440
16 Column totals	1,099	566	915	3,084	1,488	2,497	1,115	1,239	543	5,076	2,999	11,944	3,838	1,932	3,289	..

Key to column headings (horizontal)

1 Agriculture, forestry and fishing	5 Textiles, leather and clothing	9 Gas, electricity and water	13 Government appropriation
2 Mining and quarrying	6 Food, drink and tobacco	10 Other production and trade*	14 Capital transactions
3 Chemicals and allied trades	7 Other manufacturing	11 Other industries†	15 External
4 Metals, engineering and vehicles	8 Building and contracting	12 Business and households appropriation	16 Row totals

* Transport and communication, distributive trades, insurance, banking and finance, and other services.

† Public administration and defence, public health and educational services, ownership of dwellings, domestic services to households, and services to private non-profit making bodies.

CHAPTER 11

The Input-output Model and Applications

11.1 The Open Leontief Model

We now use our illustrative empirical transactions matrix (Table 10.1) for a theoretical model which purports to explain or predict the effect of any change in final demand upon sector outputs or the allocation of inputs. The pioneer of this type of model is Wassily Leontief who made, as early as 1931, an attempt to give quantitative form to the abstract, mathematical theory of general economic equilibrium which had been developed, towards the end of the last century, by Léon Walras and his disciples.

In order to follow Leontief's work we require some new symbols:

V_r = value of total output of the r-th sector among n sectors,
v_{rs} = value of intermediate goods sold by the r-th sector to the s-th sector,
v_r = value of final output sold by the r-th sector.

These symbols can be used to express the identity that total sales are all intermediate sales plus final sales,

$$(1) \qquad V_r = \sum_{s=1}^{n} v_{rs} + v_r$$

which, applied to our illustrative transactions matrix gives,

$$V_1 = v_{11} + v_{12} + v_{13} + v_1 = 69 + 136 + 0 + 95 = 300$$
$$V_2 = v_{21} + v_{22} + v_{23} + v_2 = 51 + 612 + 237 + 800 = 1{,}700$$
$$V_3 = v_{31} + v_{32} + v_{33} + v_3 = 30 + 255 + 110 + 605 = 1{,}000.$$

110

We also need corresponding symbols for prices and quantities, p_r, X_r, x_{rs} and x_r. They are related to the value symbols by the further identities,

(2) $$V_r = p_r X_r$$

(3) $$X_r = \sum_{s=1}^{n} x_{rs} + x_r^{\bullet}.$$

For the moment, we shall suppose that all prices are constant and arbitrarily set at unity, so that values can be taken as coinciding with quantities.

The crucial assumption made by Leontief is that inputs are fixed proportions of outputs – that there are fixed 'technical coefficients' of production. If so, and if prices are all constant, then these technical coefficients may be found by dividing the total for any column of the transactions matrix into the purchases of inputs that enter this column. Applying the procedure to our illustrative transactions matrix (Table 10.1) we obtain the following matrix of input-output coefficients called a 'technology matrix'.

Table 11.1 Technology Matrix

		Primary Industry 1	Secondary Industry 2	Tertiary Industry 3
1	Primary industry	·230	·080	...
2	Secondary industry	·170	·360	·237
3	Tertiary industry	·100	·150	·110
4a	Wages	·133	·200	·370
4b	Profits	·300	·023	·120
5	Net Expenditure taxes	·020	·050	·039
6	Capital consumption	·027	·046	·038
7	Imports	·020	·090	·086
		1·000	1·000	1·000

These technical coefficients are denoted by a's:

a_{rs} = input of the r-th sector's product per unit of the s-th sector's output, or the marginal input coefficient of the s-th sector with respect to the r-th sector's product.

111

Since the coefficients relate to production requirements, they should be in physical terms, i.e.

(4)
$$a_{rs} = \frac{x_{rs}}{X_s}$$

We have derived them, however, as,

$$a_{rs} = \frac{v_{rs}}{V_s} \frac{p_r}{p_s} \frac{x_{rs}}{X_s}$$

so that, clearly, our derivation is satisfactory only if relative prices remain constant; otherwise we should have to make an adjustment for changes of prices.

The first form of Leontief's model is simply the use of the definitional relation (3) together with the assumption (4), i.e.

(5)
$$X_r = \sum_{s=1}^{n} x_{rs} = x_r^*$$

(6)
$$x_{rs} = a_{rs} X_s$$

to obtain the n equations

(7)
$$X_r - \sum_{s=1}^{n} a_{rs} X_s = x_r^*.$$

The final outputs, x_r^*, are treated as predetermined so that these n equations, all linear, suffice to determine the n outputs, X_s, and so the n inputs, x_{rs}.[1]

Our illustration then becomes,

(7a)
$$\begin{aligned}
X_1 - \cdot230X_1 - 080X_2 &= x_1 = 95 \\
X_2 - \cdot170X_1 - \cdot360X_2 - \cdot237X_3 &= x_2 = 800 \\
X_3 - \cdot100X_1 - \cdot150X_2 - \cdot110X_3 &= x_3 = 605
\end{aligned}$$

or, more neatly,

---

[1] The model, for cases where there are many sectors, has to be handled by matrix algebra. Let X be the vector of outputs, x the vector of final demands, A that part of the technology matrix which applies to goods, and I the identity matrix. The model may then be written as:
$$X - AX = (I - A) X = x^*$$
corresponding to (7) or (7b). It has the solution:
$$X = (I - A)^{-1} x^*$$
so that the solution requires the (usually tedious) inversion of the matrix $(I - A)$.

$$\begin{aligned}
&\cdot770X_1 - \cdot080X_2 && = x_1 = 95 \\
\text{(7b)} \quad &- \cdot170X_1 + \cdot640X_2 - \cdot237X_3 &&= x_2 = 800 \\
&- \cdot100X_1 - \cdot150X_2 + \cdot890X_3 &&= x_3 = 605.
\end{aligned}$$

There are three outputs to determine, X_1, X_2 and X_3, and three linear equations to do this. Solving by ordinary methods we obtain

$$\text{(8)} \quad \begin{aligned}
X_1 &= 1\cdot34451x_1 + \cdot17925x_2 + \cdot04777x_3 = 300 \\
X_2 &= \cdot44091x_1 + 1\cdot72528x_2 + \cdot45979x_3 = 1{,}700 \\
X_3 &= \cdot22533x_1 + \cdot31095x_2 + 1\cdot20640x_3 = 1{,}000
\end{aligned}$$

We can, of course, then proceed to find the various intermediate inputs, and so get back to the point from which we started.

$$\text{(9)} \quad \begin{aligned}
x_{11} &= a_{11}X_1 = \cdot230X_1 = 69 \\
x_{21} &= a_{21}X_1 = \cdot170X_1 = 51 \\
x_{31} &= a_{31}X_1 = \cdot100X_1 = 30 \\
x_{12} &= a_{12}X_2 = \cdot080X_2 = 136. \\
x_{22} &= a_{22}X_2 = \cdot360X_2 = 612 \\
x_{32} &= a_{32}X_2 = \cdot150X_2 = 255 \\
x_{13} &= a_{13}X_3 = \cdot000X_3 = 0 \\
x_{23} &= a_{23}X_3 = \cdot237X_3 = 237 \\
x_{33} &= a_{33}X_3 = \cdot110X_3 = 110.
\end{aligned}$$

The coefficients in equation (8) should be contrasted with those appearing in the technology matrix. Technical coefficients give *direct requirements* of inputs per unit of sector output. The coefficients in (8) give *direct and indirect requirements* of inputs per unit of final demand. An increase, for example, of £1 in the final demand for secondary output will make for a direct increase of £1 in that output and, because of associated input requirements, for an increase of £0·080 in primary output, an increase of £0·150 in tertiary output and a further increase of £0·360 in secondary output. But these consequential expansions of sector outputs, to provide the required inputs for secondary industry, will themselves require inputs from the other sectors, these further inputs, and so on. The coefficients in (8) give the total of all such direct and indirect requirements. Thus the expansion of £1 in final demand for secondary output means an expansion, not of £1 + £·360, but one of £1·72528; at the same time, it means an expansion of £0·44091 in primary output with one of £0·45979 in tertiary output.

11.2 Requirements for Labour and Imports

So far we have derived from the set of final demands only demands for intermediate inputs. But we can also derive demands for primary inputs, and it is particularly helpful to do this for labour or for imports.

From Table 11.1 we have direct requirements for labour, per £100 of sector output, as

Sector 1 13·3,   Sector 2 20·0,   Sector 3 37·0.

The corresponding requirements for imports are

Sector 1 2·0,   Sector 2 9·0,   Sector 3 8.6.

We wish, however, to find also the total requirements, direct and indirect, per £100 of sector final demand, and find this by applying the above direct requirements to the coefficients of equation (8). Thus the total requirements for labour (assuming wages are constant), per £100 of final demand for primary output is,

$$13·3 \ (1·34451) + 20·0 \ (·44091) \ + 37·0 \ \ (·22533) = 35·0$$

the corresponding requirements for secondary output is,

$$13·3 \ (·17925) + 20·0 \ (1·72528) + 37·0 \ \ (·31095) = 48·4$$

and for tertiary output,

$$13·3 \ (·04777) \ + 20·0 \ (·45979) \ + 37·0 \ (1·20640) = 54·5$$

It is evident that a given expansion of final demand for tertiary output makes the heaviest demand for labour, and a given expansion of final demand for primary output and least demand for labour.

In a similar way we can estimate requirements for imports. The direct requirements per £100 of sector output are:

Sector 1 2·0.   Sector 2 9·0,   Sector 3 8.6

and the totals of direct and indirect requirements per £100 of sector final demand are

Sector 1   2·0 (1·34451) + 9·0   (·44091) + 8·6   (·22533) =   8·6
Sector 2   2·0   (·17925) + 9·0 (1·72528) + 8·6   (·31095) = 18·6
Sector 3   2·0   (·04777) + 9·0   (·45979) + 8·6 (1·20640) = 14·6

It is here evident that secondary production makes the most intense demand on imports and primary production the least.

Results such as these are often put into a reference table; viz.

Table 11.2 Direct and Total Requirements for Labour and Imports

Sector	Direct Requirements per £100 of Output		Total Requirements per £100 of Final Demand	
	Labour	Imports	Labour	Imports
1	13·3	2·0	35·0	8·6
2	20·0	9·0	48·4	18·6
3	27·0	8·6	54·5	14·6

11.3 Effects of Changes in Final Demands

So far we have taken the given set of final demands in Table 11.1 as the initial set in our illustrative transactions matrix and simply come back on our tracks. But the Leontief model has a main use in estimating the effects of changes in final demands.

Consider, for example, a situation where a government decides to take measures for defence which will more than double current government spending but, at the same time, in order to preserve economic stability, takes steps to reduce personal consumption and, to a lesser extent, capital formation and exports. The new structure of final demand is that given in the north-east quadrant of a new transactions matrix, Table 11.3.

We may fill in the remainder of this new matrix by estimating, first, new sector outputs. That is done by inserting the new sector final demands in equation (8):

$X_1 = 1·34451 (75) + ·17925 (775) + ·04777 (650) = 271$
$X_2 = ·44091 (75) + 1·72528 (775) + ·45979 (650) = 1,669$
$X_3 = ·22533 (75) + ·31095 (775) + 1·20640 (650) = 1,042.$

115

Table 11.3 New Matrix of Production Accounts

Inputs ↓ / Outputs →	1	2	3	A	4	5	6	7	B	C
1 Primary industry	62	134	...	196	20	...	5	50	75	271
2 Secondary industry	46	601	247	896	450	100	95	130	775	1,669
3 Tertiary industry	27	250	115	398	230	300	100	20	650	1,042
4 Factor payments:										
a) Wages	36	334	385	...	...	...	...	...	...	755
b) Profits	82	38	125	...	...	...	...	...	...	245
5 Net expenditure taxes	5	84	41	...	...	...	...	...	...	130
6 Capital consumption allowances	7	77	40	...	...	...	...	...	...	124
7 Imports, etc.	5	150	90	...	...	...	...	...	...	245
Total inputs	271	1,669	1,042	1,490	700	400	200	200	1,500	

Key to column headings (horizontal)

1	Primary industry	5	Government income account
2	Secondary industry	6	National capital account
3	Tertiary industry	7	Exports, etc.
A	Total intermediate outputs	B	Total final output
4	Personal income account	C	Total output

One consequence of the new policy is thus seen to be a 10 per cent fall in primary output, a 2 per cent fall in secondary output and a 4 per cent increase of tertiary output (which includes defence). These outputs are also inserted in the new matrix.

The next step is to apply each column of technical coefficients in Table 11.1 to the corresponding sector output in order to fill in the output column for that sector. After this has been done we see that labour has to be redistributed in accordance with the new sector outputs, and that the new structure of final demand is unbelievably successful in regard to stabilization in so far as net domestic incomes remain steady at 1,000. It has led to a small increase of wages together with a small decrease of profits, while leaving net expenditure tax receipts, capital consumption allowances and imports unchanged in totals.

116

11.4 Price Analysis

The Leontief model may be further adapted so as to provide a theory of price determination. We have used p_r, x_{rs} and a_{rs} to denote the price of the r-th commodity, the quantity of this used as an input by the s-th sector, and the (fixed) ratio of this input to the sector's output. We now introduce symbols for primary inputs; k_s denotes the average cost of all primary inputs for the s-th sector, π_i the price of the i-th input among primary inputs, and a_{is} the (fixed) requirement of this input per unit of s-th sector's output.

Reading, then, a transactions matrix downwards by columns we have the following expressions for sector costs:

$$\text{(10)} \qquad V_s = \sum_{r=1}^{n} v_{rs} + k_s X_s$$

or

$$\text{(11)} \qquad p_s X_s = \sum_{r=1}^{n} a_{rs} p_r X_s + k_s X_s$$

or

$$\text{(12)} \qquad p_s = \sum_{r=1}^{n} a_{rs} p_r + k_s$$

and

$$\text{(13)} \qquad k_s = \sum_{i=1}^{m} a_{is} \pi_i.$$

Equations (12) and (13) mean that the price of any commodity equals the sum of the products of unit input requirements and input prices. The theory, therefore, is that prices are cost-determined.

Applying (12) and (13) to our illustrative example we have, from Table 11.1,

$$\text{(14)} \qquad \begin{aligned} p_1 &= \cdot230p_1 + \cdot170p_2 + \cdot100p_3 + k_1 \\ p_2 &= \cdot080p_1 + \cdot360p_2 + \cdot150p_3 + k_2 \\ p_3 &= \qquad\quad \cdot273p_2 + \cdot110p_3 + k_3 \end{aligned}$$

and

$$\begin{aligned} k_1 &= \cdot133\pi_1 + \cdot300\pi_2 + \cdot020\pi_3 + \cdot027\pi_4 + \cdot020\pi_5 \\ k_2 &= \cdot200\pi_1 + \cdot023\pi_2 + \cdot050\pi_3 + \cdot046\pi_4 + \cdot090\pi_5 \\ k_3 &= \cdot370\pi_1 + \cdot120\pi_2 + \cdot039\pi_3 + \cdot038\pi_4 + \cdot086\pi_5 \end{aligned}$$

where

$\pi_1 =$ wage rates $\qquad\qquad$ $\pi_4 =$ unit rate of depreciation
$\pi_2 =$ unit profit margin $\qquad$ $\pi_5 =$ import prices.
$\pi_3 =$ rate of net expenditure taxes

If all prices of primary inputs are equal to unity, for a base year common to all index numbers, then

$$k_1 = \cdot500, \; k_2 = \cdot409, \; k_3 = \cdot653.$$

We could thus rearrange (13) as

$$
\begin{aligned}
(15) \quad & \cdot770p_1 - \cdot170p_2 - \cdot100p_3 = \cdot500 \\
& \cdot080p_1 + \cdot640p_2 - \cdot150p_3 = \cdot409 \\
& \qquad\quad - \cdot273p_2 + \cdot885p_3 = \cdot653.
\end{aligned}
$$

These three simultaneous, linear equations suffice to determine the three commodity prices,[1] and give them as

$$
\begin{aligned}
(16) \quad & p_1 = 1\cdot34451\,(\cdot500) + \;\;\cdot44091\,(\cdot409) + \;\;\cdot22533\,(\cdot653) = 1 \\
& p_2 = \;\;\cdot17925\,(\cdot500) + 1\cdot72528\,(\cdot409) + \;\;\cdot31095\,(\cdot653) = 1 \\
& p_3 = \;\;\cdot04777\,(\cdot500) + \;\;\cdot45979\,(\cdot409) + 1\cdot20640\,(\cdot653) = 1.
\end{aligned}
$$

11.5 Effects of Change in Wages Rates or Import Prices

This pricing model may be useful for forecasting the effects of a given change in the price of any primary input. Suppose, as a first example, the wage rates rise by 10 per cent. Then our new k's would be

$$k_1 = \cdot513, \; k_2 = \cdot429, \; k_3 = \cdot690.$$

If these new values are inserted in equation (16) we obtain,

$$p_1 = 1\cdot034, \; p_2 = 1\cdot047, \; p_3 = 1\cdot054.$$

We see, accordingly, that whereas a 10 per cent rise of wage rates would increase the price-level for primary output directly by 1·33 per cent it will, after all indirect effects through structural

---

[1] The general form of this price model is, using matrix notation,

$$p' = k' + p'A$$

or $\qquad\qquad p = k + A'p \qquad\qquad$ i.e. $(I-A)'p = k$
$$p = (I'-A')^{-1}k.$$

Note that the matrix of price coefficients is the transpose of the matrix of technical coefficients.

interdependence are allowed for, raise this price level by 3·4 per cent. For the secondary sector the direct price increase would be 2·0 per cent and the direct and indirect increase 4·7 per cent; the corresponding increases for the tertiary sector are 3·7 per cent and 5·4 per cent.

The effects of wage change may be compared with those of a 10 per cent rise of import prices. Such a rise alters k's to

$$k_1 = \cdot502, \ k_2 = \cdot418, \ k_3 = \cdot662.$$

Inserting these values in equation (16) yields new values for the p's

$$p_1 = 1\cdot008, \ p_2 = 1\cdot017, \ p_3 = 1\cdot015.$$

Increases of ·8 per cent, 1·7 per cent and 1·5 per cent compare with direct increases of ·2 per cent, ·9 per cent and ·86 per cent.

It is, again, convenient to summarize such results in a table.

Table 11.4 Effects of a 10 per cent Rise in Wage Rates or Import Prices Upon Commodity Prices

Sector Prices	Wages		Imports	
	Direct Rise	Total Rise	Direct Rise	Total Rise
	p.c.	p.c.	p.c.	p.c.
Primary industry	1·3	3·4	·2	·8
Secondary industry	2·0	4·7	·9	1·7
Tertiary industry	3·7	5·4	·9	1·5

11.6 The Role of Input-Output Analysis

Leontief's open model, described above, is obviously complementary to our earlier macro-models which, as we have seen, may be used either for forecast purposes or for policy purposes. When used for forecasting they give predictions of some final demands, e.g. personal consumption and private investment, on the assumption that other final demands, e.g. government spending and exports, are independently predicted. If to all this we add an assumption about the distribution of final demands over the various productive sectors, e.g. that they are

119

so distributed in fixed proportions, then we may proceed, by means of the Leontief model, to obtain further predictions of sector outputs and inputs, including sector demands for labour and imports. If, moreover, our macro-model has an equation giving prices as cost-determined, then we may also use the Leontief model for obtaining predictions of the effects of changes in wage-rates or import prices (taking either to be exogenous), upon sector prices or upon more general price indexes derived from sector prices.

When macro-models are used for policy purposes we take some previously forecast variables as targets, e.g. employment, prices and the balance of external trade. We then use the macro-model to estimate required values for policy variables such as government spending, taxes, wage-rates or the exchange rate. The postulated final demands together with the estimate of required final demands (mainly government spending) leads to a definite 'bill of goods'. Making the same kind of assumption about the distribution of these final demands over various sectors, we can use the Leontief model to see how the policy measures affect sector outputs and inputs, especially demands for labour and imports. When this is done, we may see that the policy measures would put impossible strains upon some sectors, and that bottlenecks could, accordingly, develop to prevent the policy measures from being fully successful. The Leontief model, that is, may point to the need for a revision of targets, or for some additional policy measures to make them more feasible.

These, and further points, are made by the Netherlands Central Planning Bureau[1]:

The macro-model has already given the total consumption, investments and exports. . . . Thus the level of final demand of the various branches of industry is known. By means of the 'input-output' method it is then also possible to determine the interindustry relations and imports corresponding thereto, by which, finally, the total output pattern is established.

Now bottlenecks were found to occur. The required increase in

[1] *Scope and Methods of the Central Planning Bureau*, (1956), pp. 47–48.

120

output of agriculture and mining appeared . . . to be greater than could reasonably be deemed possible. Under such circumstances extra imports are required . . .

The pattern of production which can be established in this way furnishes the basis for further analysis: the pattern of employment, the training programme, the investment pattern and the like are deduced therefrom.

In this connexion it is necessary that agreement exists between the totals according to the macro-analysis and 'input-output' analysis. As such, the latter can contribute to a verification and, possibly, revision of the coefficients used in the macro-model.

11.7 Limitations of the Analysis

Input-output analysis is a comparatively new study and one which is especially dependent upon full or detailed data. It is not, therefore, surprising that it has been slowly applied, that some applications have not been very successful, nor that input-output analysts have called for fuller or more systematic compilation of industrial data to meet their needs. There would, however, probably be general enough agreement that it has proved a promising tool, and that it should be further developed.

A thorough study of the practical success of the input-output approach was made by Hatanaka,[1] based upon a 1947 U.S. table for 30 industries. Final demands, of later years, were applied to the technology matrix to get estimates of sector outputs. These estimates were compared, not only with actual sector outputs, but also with different estimates based upon 30 multiple-regression equations having GNP and time as independent variables over the period 1929–40 and 1946–8. Average weighted percentage errors were considerably less for input-output estimates than for the regression estimates, both for short-run projections of 1–2 years and for long-run projections of 7–10 years.

There are, of course, many other results which speak in favour of input-output analysis, and they could well be better

---

[1] Quoted: H. B. Chenery and P. G. Clark, *Interindustry Economics*, (1959), pp. 173–6.

with more adequate data. But fundamental doubts are raised by the basic assumptions of the whole analysis; viz.

(i) Each sector has a single output and uses only one method of producing it
(ii) Each input is strictly proportional to the sector's output
(iii) Total output is the sum-total of sector outputs.

The first assumption would preclude joint production (unless joint products can be treated as a single composite commodity), the second assumption rules out substitution between inputs in response to changes in their relative prices, and the third assumption, implying constant returns to scale, rules out external economies or diseconomies. At best, these assumptions can hold only approximately.

Part Four
Policy Problems

CHAPTER 12

Can the Economy Regulate Itself?

12.1 The Ricardo-Wicksell Model

The basic question in economic policy is the extent to which a market economy, however 'mixed', can be relied upon to keep the aggregate demand for commodities in balance with their aggregate supply, and so avoid either unemployment or inflation. If an economy had strong enough tendencies to preserve equilibrium at full employment levels, and to correct deviations promptly, there would obviously be little need for macroeconomic policy. It might seem that, because governments are now committed to apply such policy, the system cannot be self-regulating. But this commitment was the result of the Great Depression and it is difficult to believe that, since then, economic disasters have been everywhere avoided only because of bold and skilful government action. The most plausible view is a middle one; the system must have marked tendencies towards equilibrium but they are probably neither sufficiently reliable nor prompt to dispense with some need for proper corrective action.

Economists whom Keynes described as 'classical' emphasized, perhaps too much, automatic stabilisers, in particular the role of interest in adjusting investment to saving. The following model has been used[1] to represent their views in a concise way, and comes close to the analysis Wicksell[2] made on the basis of some strong hints of Ricardo.[3]

[1] See, e.g. D. Patinkin, Ch. 5 of *Post-Keynesian Economics* (edited by K. Kurihara); L. Klein, *The Keynesian Revolution*, pp. 199–206.

[2] K. Wicksell, *Lectures on Political Economy*, Vol. II, pp. 175–208.

[3] D. Ricardo, *The High Price of Bullion*, esp. p. 22.

Employment is supposed to be determined by the labour market. The ordinary theory of demand, when leisure is treated as a good, indicates a rising supply curve for labour (at least up to the point where the income effect of a wage increase swamps the substitution effect to make the curve backward sloping). The theory of profit maximization leads to a downward sloping demand curve, because of diminishing marginal returns, so that there will be an equilibrium level of employment corresponding to the intersection of the two curves.

Algebraically we have:

$$(1.1) \quad N^s = f\left(\frac{w}{p}\right) \qquad\qquad f' > 0$$

$$(1.2) \quad N^d = \phi\left(\frac{w}{p}\right) \qquad\qquad \phi' < 0$$

$$(1.3) \quad N^f = N^d = N^s$$

where w and p denote levels of money wages and prices, and f' or ϕ' is a first derivative. Geometrically, we have

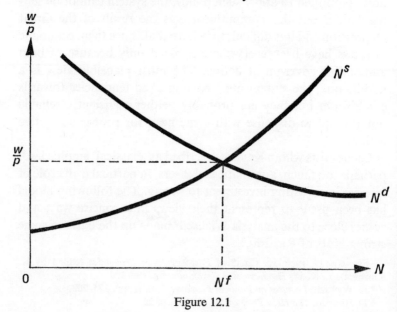

Figure 12.1

126

Here ON^f represents full employment because, if the supply curve is rising, no one wishing to work at the ruling wage, $\dfrac{w}{p}$, fails to obtain a job.

This equilibrium level of employment, applied to a production function that is seriously defective in ignoring the effect of capital,

$$(1.4) \quad Y = Y(N)$$

gives the full employment aggregate supply of goods, Y^f.

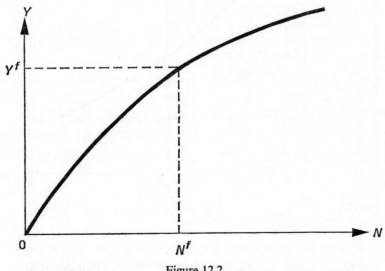

Figure 12.2

The aggregate demand for goods, Z, is taken to increase with real income or output, Y, and to decrease with the rate of interest, r, a rise of which checks both investment and consumption.

$$(1.5) \quad Z = Z(Y, r) \qquad\qquad Z_Y > 0, Z_r < 0.$$

But, as income has just been determined at Y^f, it must be

127

interest which brings aggregate demand into balance with aggregate supply;

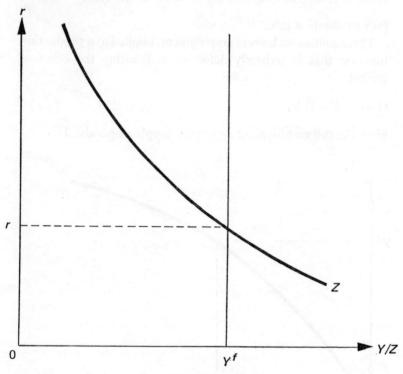

Figure 12.3

If, then, the labour market determines the real wage, employment, and hence output, it is the goods market that determines the rate of interest which, therefore, may be regarded as a 'real' phenomenon. We can express the same idea by saying that interest is determined by saving and investment; for

$$Z = C + I = Y$$

means that

$$Y - C = S = I$$

and if consumption, as well as investment, decreases as interest rises, saving must increase.

128

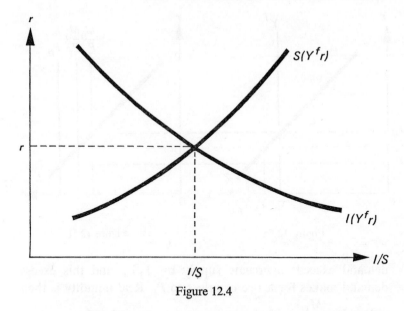

Figure 12.4

There is, finally, the money market to consider. The supply of money may be regarded as fixed by the authorities, but the demand for liquidity, like the demand for goods, increases with income and decreases as interest rises, i.e.

$$(1.6) \qquad \frac{M^*}{P} = L(Y, r), \qquad\qquad L_Y > 0, L_r < 0.$$

Since, however, income has been determined by the labour market, and interest by the goods market, all that remains for the money market is to determine the price level, P, which is seen as proportionate to the quantity of money.

But all this presupposes equilibrium adjustments, which take time to work out. The nature of adjustment to an increased quantity of money is shown in the following diagram.

There is equilibrium, initially, in both the goods market and the money market, with interest r_0. The quantity of money then increases from M_0 to M_1, but the price level lags behind, remaining for a while at P_0. The real value of liquid balances increases, therefore, and interest falls to r_1. But at r_1 aggregate

129

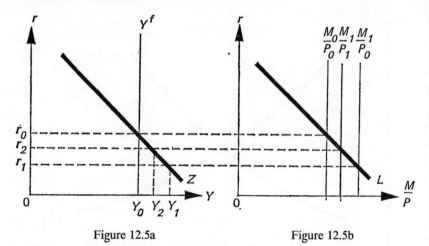

Figure 12.5a   Figure 12.5b

demand exceeds aggregate supply by $Y_1 Y_0$, and this excess demand makes for a rise of prices to P_1. Real liquidity is then reduced to $\dfrac{M_1}{P_1}$, so that interest rises to r_2, and reduces excess demand to $Y_0 Y_2$. There is still some excess demand and so a further, but smaller, rise of prices which again reduces liquidity and raises interest higher. The process goes on until interest has risen sufficiently to restore equilibrium between aggregate demand and aggregate supply. In the end, therefore, interest is fixed by the goods market, although temporarily disturbed by the money market, and the only permanent effect of the greater quantity of money is to raise prices.

All this illustrates Ricardo's remark:

It is only during the interval of the issues of the Bank, and their effect on prices, that we should be sensible of an abundance of money; interest would, during that interval, be under its natural level; but as soon as the additional . . . money became absorbed . . . interest would be high.

It also explains Wicksell's general principle[1]:

At any moment and in any economic situation there is always a certain rate of interest at which the . . . general level of commodity

[1] *Selected Papers on Economic Theory*, (edited by E. Lindahl), pp. 82–3.

prices (has) no tendency to change. This can be called the *normal rate of interest.* . . . If the rate of interest on money deviates downwards . . . from this normal level prices will, as long as the deviation lasts, rise continuously; if it deviates upwards, they will fall indefinitely in the same way.

12.2 Keynes's Critique

Keynes was most critical of this classical theory in regard to the labour market.[1] He accepted the demand curve for labour but rejected the analysis from which the supply curve of labour was derived. The wage rate, he held, was not so much determined by the market as fixed by collective bargaining. Such bargaining, of course, fixes a money wage but, to the extent that prices are cost-determined and that costs depend upon wages, prices will also be fixed and hence a real as well as a money wage. At this wage a large number of workers would accept employment, say ON_2 in Fig. 12.6, but demand for labour may be only ON_1, leaving N_1N_2 workers 'involuntarily' unemployed.

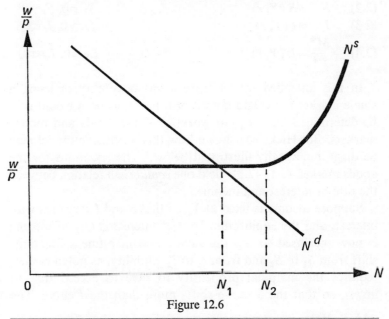

Figure 12.6

---

[1] J. M. Keynes, *The General Theory of Employment, Interest and Money,* Ch. 2.

131

Nor would a wage cut necessarily correct the situation; prices might fall with money wages so that the real wage rate is little changed, and falling prices might so disturb business expectations as to make for a fall in the demand for labour, thus aggravating unemployment. The only sure remedy lies in raising the demand for labour, not in cutting wages.

There has been much discussion about this criticism, and we shall later have to consider a more sophisticated analysis of the labour market which takes account of Keynes's points. For the moment, however, we need only notice that, if accepted, it makes unnecessary any general consideration of the labour market. If money wages are fixed by collective bargaining and prices are adjusted to wages, two variables may be taken as given and so two equations dropped from the model, viz. those representing demand for and supply of labour. This Keynesian purging would reduce the previous model to:

(2.1) $\quad Z \;= C+I= Y$ or $Y-C=S=I$

(2.2) $\quad S \;=S\,(Y,r)$ $\hspace{4cm}$ $S_Y>0, S_r>0$

(2.3) $\quad I \;=I\,(Y,r)$ $\hspace{4cm}$ $I_Y >0, I_r <0$

(2.4) $\quad \dfrac{M^*}{P^*}=L\,(Y,r)$ $\hspace{3.5cm}$ $L_Y>0, L_r<0.$

In this amended model there is no possibility of using a single market to explain output or interest, as both would now be determined by the joint working of the goods and money markets. But Hicks has shown how this Keynesian model may be diagrammatically illustrated below.[1] The equations for the goods market, (2.1)–(2.3), yield one *equilibrium* relation between the rate of interest and income.

Suppose income is fixed at Y_1, so that S and I vary only with interest, and the equilibrium level of interest is Or_1. If income is now increased to Y_2, the saving and investment functions shift from S_1 to S_2 and from I_1 to I_2. Stability, as noted earlier, requires the marginal propensity to save to exceed that to invest, so that the S curve shifts more than the I curve. The

[1] J. R. Hicks, *Econometrica*, 1937, reprinted as Ch. 24 of *Readings in the Theory of Income Distribution.*

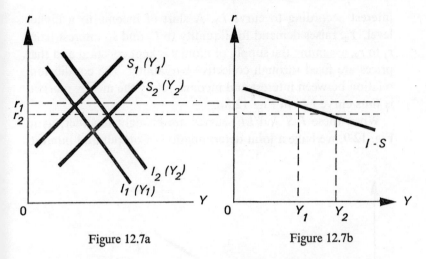

Figure 12.7a   Figure 12.7b

new intersection then gives an equilibrium rate of interest, Or_2, below the old rate. By other variations of income we can thus generate the I–S curve in Fig. 12.7b, showing the relation set by the goods market between *equilibrium* rates of interest and income.

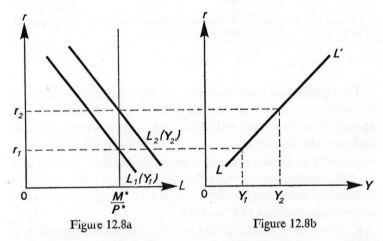

Figure 12.8a   Figure 12.8b

The money market gives another such equilibrium relation between interest and income.

If income is held at Y_1, liquidity preference varies with interest according to curve L_1. A shift of income to a higher level, Y_2, raises demand for liquidity to L_2 and so interest from r_1 to r_2, assuming the supply of money is kept constant and that prices are fixed through collective bargaining. The equilibrium relation between interest and income, set by the money market, is thus curve LL' in Fig. 12.8b.

When these I–S and LL' curves are brought together, as in Fig. 12.9, we have a joint determination of output and interest.

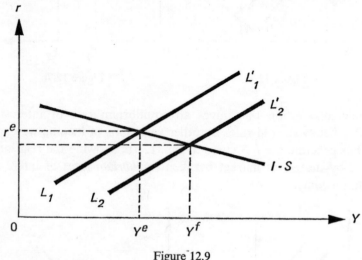

Figure 12.9

The equilibrium level of output, Y^e, thus determined need not, of course, be a full employment level, Y^f. But interest still appears to be the means of keeping the goods market in balance, and now the money market also. Monetary policy, moreover, appears to be an adequate instrument for adjusting the system to full employment levels; for if the supply of money is sufficiently increased to shift $L_1 L_1'$ to $L_2 L'$ then the level of output will rise from OY^e to OY^f.

Keynes's second main criticism called these comfortable conclusions into question. He uses here the idea of a 'liquidity trap', explained earlier; if there is some minimum rate of interest at which the demand for liquidity becomes virtually absolute, the L curves in Fig. 12.8b become horizontal at this minimum rate, and Fig. 12.9 becomes:

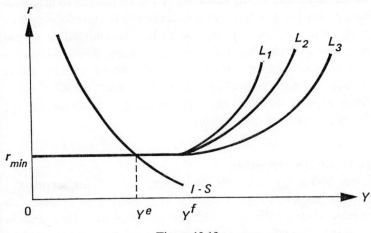

Figure 12.10

Any increase in the quantity of money, shifting the LL' curve from L_1 to L_2, or even to L_3, will be powerless to shift Y^e towards Y^f if the I–S curve intersects the LL' curve along its horizontal stretch.

Keynes, it is true, did not assert this as more than a possibility. Patinkin, however, has denied that it is a possibility which can damage monetary policy.[1] Increases in the quantity of money (without corresponding increases of government spending) require purchases of bonds by the central banks from other financial institutions or from the public. If such a policy is continued long enough, the central bank must sooner or later acquire all holdings of bonds and completely saturate the speculative demand for money because the public no longer has the possibility of substituting between money and bonds. The rate of interest would fall to zero and, as it fell, would obviously lead to an increase of output along the I–S curve. As Hicks points out[2] however, and as Patinkin himself seems to recognize,

[1] D. Patinkin, *Money, Interest and Prices*, pp. 245–9.
[2] J. R. Hicks, *Economic Journal*, 1957.

135

if the central bank pushed matters to this extreme, it would take over all bond holdings of financial intermediaries, without which they could hardly function, and so be obliged to take over all their lending and borrowing functions to the public! Keynes's doctrine of the liquidity trap has to be reformulated; it should be taken to mean that there may be a limit below which the central bank cannot push the rate of interest without either leading to economic chaos through a breakup of existing financial institutions, or else without completely socializing the financial sector of the economy.

12.3 Klein's Scepticism

Klein had a far more thoroughgoing ground for scepticism, both in respect to the tendency of a market to achieve full employment equilibrium without government action and in respect to the efficacy of monetary policy. Although regarding himself as a Keynesian, he adopted classical views about demand for labour or its supply, and rejected Keynes's idea of a liquidity trap. Contrary, however, to Robertson[1] who thought that in Keynes's work, 'roughly speaking, nothing was ever allowed to happen – money was not allowed to affect prices, wage rates were not allowed to affect employment, I had almost added, the moon was not allowed to affect the tides – except through the rate of interest', Klein[2] found that, whereas 'the classical theory . . . assumes that savings decisions and investment decisions both respond sensitively to the rate of interest . . . Keynesian economics assumes that both functions are interest-inelastic'.

Klein thus reached a simplified form of Keynes's model.

$$(3.1) \qquad S = S(Y)$$

$$(3.2) \qquad I = I(Y)$$

$$(3.3) \qquad \frac{M^*}{P} = L(r, Y).$$

[1] D. H. Robertson, *Utility and All That*, (1952), p. 83.
[2] L. R. Klein, *The Keynesian Revolution*, (1950), p. 202.

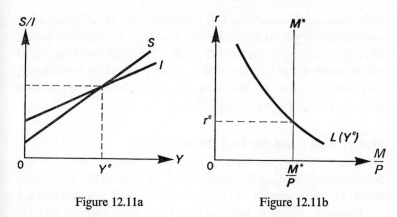

Figure 12.11a   Figure 12.11b

Here, income is determined by the equilibrium of saving and investment, according to the ordinary multiplier process; in other words, exclusive reliance is placed upon changes of income to produce equilibrium in the goods market. The equilibrium level of income is then substituted into the liquidity preference function so that the money market has the role only of determining interest, which now appears as a purely monetary phenomenon unconnected with those influences of thrift or productivity which underlie saving and investment.

All this, however, assumes that prices are fixed. They may be fixed, in effect, through collective bargaining which, by adjusting the wage rate, fixes cost-determined prices. But it is also possible, as during the war years and for some time afterwards, that the authorities peg the rate of interest. In that event, the money market could be seen as determining the price level; the Klein model would then, in this respect, resemble the Ricardo-Wicksell model.

In his later work with Goldberger, Klein makes the change of wages depend upon the degree of unemployment. In that case, if saving and investment led to unemployment, wages would fall and, with them, prices; the supply of liquidity would thus increase and the rate of interest would fall. Yet, so long as neither saving nor investment depends upon interest or liquidity, there could be no change in real income or employment. The

137

only means of achieving full employment, or of preventing overfull employment and inflation, would be government action to control aggregate demand through adjustments of taxes or of government spending. The task of policy would be formidable, and made harder by the lack of any automatic tendencies towards full employment equilibrium.

12.4 Patinkin and the Real Balance Effect

Patinkin has put forward powerful arguments for another possible equilibrating influence which he calls the 'real balance effect' or 'influence on demand of a change in real balances',[1] i.e. liquidity. Patinkin believes that both consumption and investment demands are influenced by holdings of liquidity or of real money balances, and traces this idea to Wicksell, Irving Fisher and the Cambridge economists, Marshall, Pigou and Robertson.[2]

Substituting this real balance effect for the interest effect in the classical model, we should have[3]:

(4.1) $\qquad N^d = \phi \left(\dfrac{w}{p}\right)$ $\qquad\qquad\qquad\qquad \phi' < 0$

(4.2) $\qquad N^s = f \left(\dfrac{w}{p}\right)$ $\qquad\qquad\qquad\qquad f' > 0$

(4.3) $\qquad N = N^s = N^d$

(4.4) $\qquad Y = Y(N)$

(4.5) $\qquad Z = C + I$

(4.6) $\qquad C = C(Y, L)$ $\qquad\qquad\qquad\qquad C_Y > 0, C_L > 0$

(4.7) $\qquad I = I(Y, L)$ $\qquad\qquad\qquad\qquad I_Y > 0, I_L > 0$

(4.8) $\qquad Y = Z$

(4.9) $\qquad \dfrac{M^*}{P} = L(r, Y)$ $\qquad\qquad\qquad\qquad L_Y > 0, L_r < 0.$

---

[1] D. Patinkin, *Money, Interest and Prices*, (1956), p. 21.
[2] op. cit., Supplementary Notes, E, F and G.
[3] cp. D. Patinkin, Ch. 5 of *Post-Keynesian Economics*, (edited by K. Kurihara).

and hence

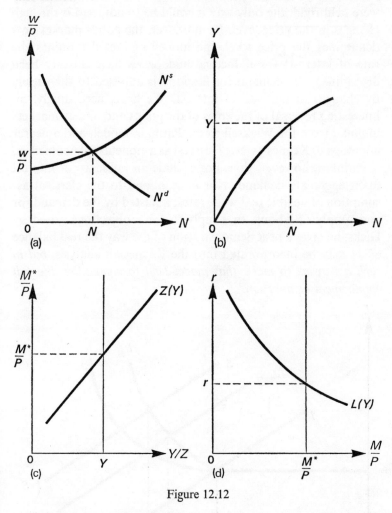

Figure 12.12

Again there is full employment, and the real wage is determined by the labour market which thus, through the production function, sets the full employment level of output or real income. But now the goods market determines the price level if aggregate demand is adjusted to the full employment supply of goods through the influence from liquidity. Liquidity should be adjusted

139

so as to bring about this balance and, if the quantity of money were held rigid, the only way it could be so adjusted is through changes in the price level. If, moreover, the goods market now determines the price level, the money market determines the rate of interest; for if income and prices have already been determined, the demand for liquidity is adjusted to the supply by changes in the rate of interest. We have, accordingly, an interesting reversal of the roles of the goods and money markets in going from the Wicksell to the Patinkin model, and a nearer approach to Keynes's view of interest as a monetary phenomenon.

Patinkin, however, does not exclude an influence of interest upon aggregate demand. Nor is he bound to the classical assumption of flexible real wage rates, adjusted by the demand for and supply of labour. In a reply to some objections raised by Hicks, he gives a neat demonstration of the way the real balance effect may be incorporated into the Keynesian analysis, *but in such a way as to make that model lead to something like full employment equilibrium.*[1]

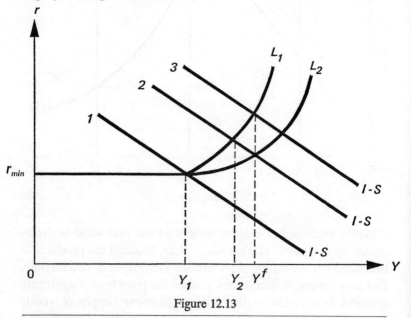

Figure 12.13

[1] D. Patinkin, *Economic Journal*, 1959, pp. 582–7.

Suppose, in the above diagram, we have a Keynesian situation of underfull employment equilibrium at output Y_1, where the *I-S* curve intersects the *LL'* curve in the region of a liquidity trap. There can, nevertheless, be an automatic, although painful, way out if we make, like Klein, the *additional assumption* that unemployment causes wages, and so prices, to fall. Such a fall, given the quantity of money, must increase liquidity and, because of the real balance effect, lead to greater demands for consumption and investment. The *I-S* curve, therefore, goes on rising so long as unemployment exerts this pressure upon prices.

At some stage the curve reaches a position, such as 2, beyond the liquidity trap. The process of falling prices, increasing liquidity and rising demands might continue until the *I-S* curve rose further to position 3, corresponding to full employment output. But another possibility is now open. The authorities can avoid further deflation by increasing the quantity of money so that the *LL'* curve shifts from L_1 to L_2, intersecting the *I-S* curve at position 2, and so reaching full employment output through monetary expansion.

12.5 Kaldor and Profit Changes

Another suggestion about an automatic tendency towards full employment has been made by Kaldor.[1] He has argued that, as periods of severe unemployment are comparatively rare and brief, the economic system must have functioned in such a way as to promote full employment or something close to it. The explanation he favours is based upon changes in the relative share of profits in the national income.

We have seen, in Chapter 4, that capitalists have a much smaller marginal propensity to consume than workers. The share of profits, moreover, tends to increase during a boom, as wages lag behind prices, and to fall during a recession, for the same reason. If, then, the system has reached a position of full employment, it will have some tendency to stay there. An upward deviation would, by increasing the share of profits, tend to reduce the general marginal propensity to consume, thus

[1] N. Kaldor, *Economica*, (1959), pp. 212 ff.

lowering aggregate demand and output. Conversely, a downward deviation, leading to a falling share of profits, tends to raise demand, output and employment. Investment, of course, has also to be considered and is likely to behave in the opposite way; for it tends to rise or fall with the level of profits and so with the share of profits in the national income. Nevertheless if, as is likely, capitalists have a greater marginal propensity to save than to invest, a rising share of profits makes for some net reduction of aggregate demand, just as a falling share of profits makes for an increase.

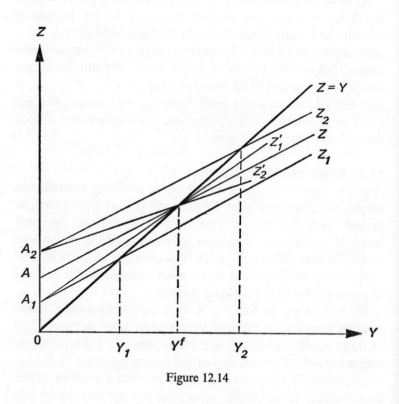

Figure 12.14

Suppose we have, initially, full employment equilibrium at Y^f. But then autonomous expenditures drop from OA to OA_1. If the

142

marginal propensity to spend were constant, the aggregate demand curve would drop from AZ to A_1Z_1 and output would fall to OY_1. But if profits fall as a proportion of income, thus increasing the marginal propensity to spend, A_1Z_1 rotates upwards, and may reach the position A_1Z_1' at which full employment is restored. Or if autonomous spending jumps to OA_2, there would be excess demand Y_2Y^f if the marginal propensity to spend were unchanged; a shift of profits, however, may wipe this out by rotating A_2Z_2 to A_2Z_2'.

12.6 The Need for Policy

Three possible mechanisms have, then, been considered for achieving full employment without special government action. It seems hard, however, in view of the empirical evidence considered in Chapters 4 and 5 to place much reliance upon the Ricardo-Wicksell mechanism of interest adjustments. Any tendency of this sort appears to be rather weak. It is most evident in regard to housing, public utilities or transportation systems but only is so far as these are not subject to public investment, which need pay little attention to interest calculations in the face of broader considerations of national or social advantage. Patinkin's real balance effect seems much more promising but here, too, there is little evidence for it.

Our earlier discussion in Chapter 4 suggested that, although there are marked differences in marginal propensities to consume of workers, farmers and capitalists, big changes in the distribution of income between these groups are needed for a marked effect upon the general marginal propensity to consume. And, as we have just noted, such changes would be partly offset by opposite changes in the propensity to invest. It seems unlikely, therefore, that this profit mechanism is strong enough to maintain full employment.

There would seem, by default, to be a good case for government action to promote or preserve full employment. We need not, however, accept Klein's earlier conclusion that everything depends upon government policy. Even if the suggested automatic mechanisms are too weak to maintain full employment, in all circumstances, they have some influence and should at least help policy to achieve this goal. Nor should we forget the possibility, noted in the discussion of models in Chapter 2, that any disturbances to the economy might lead to quickly damped cycles simply because of its structure.

CHAPTER 13

Fiscal Policy

13.1 Targets and Instruments

The need for policy has been seen to arise if the economy, left to itself, does not work satisfactorily or, if so, only after intolerable hardships and delays. Governments have thus come to accept at least a residual responsibility for ensuring that the economy fully and promptly meets the objectives of:

   (i) a high level of employment
   (ii) a reasonable rate of growth in real income per head
  (iii) reasonably stable prices
  (iv) a comfortable balance of external payments.

The list, of course, is not complete but includes all generally accepted concerns of modern economic policy.

Policy means taking action to ensure that objectives are realized. It may be more or less, better or worse, planned. Thinking in terms of national accounting, we may distinguish between three levels of macro-economic planning.

(a) *Ad hoc* policy means taking corrective action only after the national accounts, or more up-to-the-minute economic indicators, have revealed failure to meet one of the requirements listed above, e.g. a rise in unemployment. The corrective action then taken is directed more or less narrowly to remedying the particular difficulty, without taking adequate account of its repercussions upon other objectives of policy. If, for example, unemployment is met by an increase of government spending the resulting expansion of demand could worsen the balance of external payments by increasing imports.

(b) A *national budget policy*, such as has been used since the war by Scandinavian countries,[1] seeks to obtain projections of the national accounts for the coming year. If these projections indicate trouble, it may be dealt with by altering those items in the national accounts which the government can control in order to ensure all objectives are met. The projected accounts, thus revised, become not merely a forecast but a consistent and integrated set of policy measures.

(c) An *econometric decision model*, such as is used in the Netherlands, is associated with a more sophisticated type of planning. Here projections of the national accounts may be at least partly derived from an econometric model. At the same time, objectives may be translated into target values for such variables as unemployment, income, prices and the balance of payments, and the model used to estimate required values of government items for realizing the targets.

We could thus define economic policy, ideally and formally, as the control of some parameters in an econometric model, selected as *instruments*, in order to achieve *target values* of other variables corresponding to the government's basic economic objectives. The choice of instruments, of course, is limited to the variables that the state can control, and includes:

(i) fiscal measures relating to government spending, transfers and taxes
(ii) monetary measures relating to the quantity of money, interest rates, government debt operations and credit conditions
(iii) wage-controls, if the state has substantial influence over minimum or maximum wage rates
(iv) adjustment of the rate of exchange between the national currency and other currencies, and controls over external transactions.

Wage-control is most directly related to the third objective of price stability, at least to the extent that prices depend on wage rates, and controls over external transactions to the fourth objective of external solvency. It may be noted, however, that,

[1] See P. J. Bjerve, *Planning in Norway*, 1947–56, Ch. II.

although we generally need as many instruments as there are separate targets, sometimes one instrument may suffice for a number of targets. If, for example, taxes are so adjusted as to preserve full employment at a level where there is no excess demand for goods, and so no excessive demands for imports, there may be no trouble with the balance of payments.

13.2 Fiscal Instruments

Fiscal policy is often taken to refer to those items which appear in the government's fiscal budget, and so would include not only state expenditures, transfers or taxes but also government debt operations. It seems preferable, however, in view of the fact that the central bank also conducts transactions in government bonds, and co-ordinates them with new Treasury issues, to regard state debt operations as an aspect of monetary policy.

There is still a wide variety of fiscal instruments.

(i) Direct tax rates alter disposable private income and so private spending.

(ii) Indirect tax rates also affect real private income; to the extent that they are 'passed on' in higher prices, they reduce real private income as a whole and, to the extent that they are 'absorbed', reduce profits.

(iii) Rates of transfer payments can be regarded as negative direct taxes, and so have the opposite effects. If an increase of transfers is financed by higher direct taxes there are, of course, conflicting effects upon private spending, but this is likely to show some increase if those receiving the transfers have a higher marginal propensity to spend than those paying the increased direct taxes.

(iv) Rates of subsidy payments have, similarly, opposite effects upon private spending to rates of indirect tax.

(v) Current government spending on goods and services is a component of aggregate demand, and so affects this directly.

(vi) Government capital formation is also a component of

147

aggregate demand. But, in so far as investment, by increasing the stock of productive capital, makes for greater production in the future, it may be considered separately, and more directly, in relation to the second objective of economic growth. We should not, however, overlook that government capital formation may be at the expense of private capital formation, and that neither may lead to a proportional increase of productive capital, and so of productivity.

It has to be stressed[1] that the instruments of fiscal policy are *rates* of taxes, transfers and subsidies, not the corresponding *collections* of taxes or *payments* of transfers or subsidies. The government can control such rates but not the collection or payments, because these also depend upon the way income, output and employment develop, partly as a result of outside influences such as the weather, or economic conditions in other countries, affecting demands for exports or supplies of imports. *Government spending*, on goods, services or capital formation, however, may be regarded as an instrument to the extent that budget figures have to be realized.

The *budget surplus* (or deficit) cannot thus be an instrument, if only because tax collections depend upon economic developments, as well as upon tax rates. In this connection, moreover, we should note the following points:

(a) The 'balanced budget theorem' shows that, even if the budget surplus is held steady, an increase of government spending increases aggregate demand by exactly the same amount. For, if we have, as the surplus

$$G - T = 0$$

the identity

$$\Delta Y = \Delta (C + I + G)$$

and the propensities

$$C = c(Y - T)$$
$$I = i(Y - T)$$

[1] Bent Hansen, *The Economic Theory of Fiscal Policy*, (1958), Ch. II.

148

then it follows, remembering $s = 1 - c$, that

$$\Delta Y = \frac{1}{s-i} \, [\Delta G - (c+i)\, \Delta T] = \frac{1}{s-i} \, (s-i)\, \Delta G = \Delta G.$$

A balanced budget, therefore, does not guarantee stability in aggregate demand.

(b) The same target may be achieved by a variety of fiscal means, each of which could have a different effect upon the budget surplus. A £100 millions reduction of aggregate demand, for example, could be achieved by an equal reduction of government spending, but also by a rise of direct tax rates. If the marginal propensity of private spending is 0·80, then the necessary rise of tax rates would have to be sufficient to reduce private disposable income by £125 millions, and so would make for a government surplus larger by £25 millions than that resulting from the cut in spending. A rise of indirect taxes could have a still different effect upon the surplus.

(c) A budget surplus, as such, has no effect upon the calculations, and so the spending, of either the government or the private sector, but is rather the result of that spending, in so far as this depends upon liquidity and in so far as liquidity is altered by a budget surplus. Here we should remember the identity;

Current budget deficit + Government capital formation
= Net current government borrowing from the private sector
+ Money created for state spending by the central bank.

13.3 Functional Finance

Keynes was the leading advocate, in Britain, of public spending as a means of overcoming depression. As early as 1933 he had argued, in *The Means to Prosperity*, that spending on public works would increase employment, not only directly, but even more indirectly.[1] This idea was elaborated in *The General Theory of Employment, Interest and Money*, (1935), as the now familiar multiplier argument.[2] But he warned against possible adverse complications; public borrowing to finance works, by

[1] Op. cit., p. 10.
[1] Op. cit., p. 117.

pushing up interest, could discourage private investment, and deficit financing could do the same thing by upsetting business confidence.

The Swedes, however, were practising this theory before Keynes was preaching it. As Ohlin[1] wrote:

In January, 1933, the Swedish Government presented a budget proposal with an Appendix prepared by Professor Myrdal on fiscal policy and depression. . . . He advocated an attempt to create an adequate volume of aggregate demand through an increase in public works, financed through borrowing. . . . The Swedish Riksdag in the spring approved a large expansion of public works . . . The first practical result of a more permanent character of the new 'expansionist' attitude was a decision in 1937 by the Swedish Riksdag that no attempt should be made to balance the budget over a twelve-month period. There is no a priori economic reason why the state should be forced to employ a twelve-month period for balancing its accounts. The Riksdag accepted a proposal to take a business cycle as the basic period. . . . The budget normally should have a deficit in depressions and a surplus in booms. In order to prevent the Minister of Finance from forgetting the deficit in a past depression, rules were laid down that if a deficit appeared one year, he must enter 20 p.c. of that deficit as a debit item to be covered by revenue in the next year. . . . The 20 p.c. rule is not a very rational thing, of course. However, it placates the conservative opinion.

In 1944 a report was presented by a special public investment board that had been created a few years earlier in order to prepare detailed plans for public works. It had been found in the thirties that in many cases it took much time before public works could get under way. The conclusion was drawn that all the blue prints should be ready in advance. Therefore, these blue prints have been made, and now quite a large volume of public works is ready for realisation whenever a recession starts. The financial technique used was the following one: over and above the ordinary current budget and the ordinary capital investment budget, the government prepared a third, 'an emergency budget', which includes grants for all these planned extra works. The Riksdag has to pass each appropriation individually . . . but nothing is done about it until . . . the government thinks that now is the time . . . for an expansion of public investment. Then it has only to press a button and the whole things starts.

[1] B. Ohlin, *The Problem of Employment Stabilization*, (1949), pp. 65–70.

The United Nations has endorsed similar principles in its report on *National and International Measures for Full Employment* (1949).

The adaptation of the fiscal policy of the state to the needs of full employment will undoubtedly be one of the principal vehicles for stabilizing effective demand at the full-employment level in private-enterprise economies. The means for such an adaptation consists of changes in the level and kinds of expenditure, changes in the level and kinds of taxation, as well as changes in the relations between these two; and finally, in the adaptation of both taxation and expenditure to increase their flexibility in response to fluctuations in effective demand.[1]

This kind of policy has been called 'functional finance' by A. P. Lerner, one of its strongest advocates. In his *Economics of Control* (1946) he points out that governments have six effective instruments for maintaining full employment and preventing inflation: 'taxing and spending, borrowing and lending, and buying and selling'. (Buying, however, does not seem to be distinguishable from spending, and selling must be unimportant in connection with pure government activities.) Functional finance is 'the principle of disregarding all traditional conceptions of what is "sound" in finance and judging fiscal measures only by their effects or the way they function in society'. The most important of those traditional conceptions is the view that the budget must be balanced if only to avoid a ruinous growth of public debt. Lerner points out that a growth of *internal debt* is no real burden as it involves only transfer; e.g. a redistribution of income between bondholders and taxpayers. Unemployment, however, means an avoidable loss of real income so that an unbalanced budget is a very minor price to pay for full employment. Taxation, moreover, is never justified as a means of raising money for public expenditure; that could always be provided by credit creation. The real purpose of taxation is to restrict private spending, and that, too, is the real purpose of borrowing from the public by issues of government loans.

A. H. Hansen held similar views but spoke of a 'managed

[1] Op. cit., p. 76–7.

compensatory fiscal program'.[1] He laid most emphasis upon public capital expenditures and upon tax changes. Current government spending is certainly difficult to vary substantially of quickly, and it would be wrong to sacrifice normal purposes of efficiency of government to the requirements of stability. Capital expenditures, moreover, cannot be suddenly changed without long-range plans and preparations fitted into a comprehensive, varied and flexible development programme. A *flexible tax system* is thus equally necessary for an effective stabilization policy.

Just as Congress has (within limits established by law) empowered the executive to make adjustments in tariff rates, and just as Congress in the Federal Reserve Act allocated to the monetary authorities (within limits established by legislation) the power to raise and lower reserve ratios, so also it now becomes highly important, and indeed essential, to permit executive adjustment of the basic income-tax rate within limits imposed by Congress.

Arthur Smithies[2] doubted whether the President would want, or Congress grant, executive power to vary taxes. The executive, of course, can always spend less than the legislature has sanctioned, and that negative power may be a useful weapon in fighting inflation. But in order to counteract deflation by greater public spending, or inflation by higher taxes, Smithies favoured the kind of double budgeting which has been provided for in Sweden. There would be a regular budget of a long-term character, not directed towards short-term stabilization of the economy. This would be supplemented by an extraordinary budget, also ratified by Congress, involving special revenue and expenditure measures that the executive could put into force if it deemed them necessary for stability.

In 1961 the British Budget gave the Chancellor power to vary rates of indirect taxation by up to 10 per cent within the fiscal year if he should judge that economic stability required such a change. The same Budget gave power to vary employers' National Insurance contributions in a similar way so as to

[1] *Monetary Theory and Fiscal Policy*, pp. 180–3.
[2] See Ch. 5, *A Survey of Contemporary Economics* (edited by H. S. Ellis), 1948.

regulate demand for labour, but the power was quickly abandoned after strong opposition. The discretionary power of varying indirect tax rates was used in August 1961, but not thereafter. A number of countries, however, including Britain and New Zealand, have used 'mini-budgets' at different times from the normal budget date in order to make urgent fiscal changes.

13.4 Built-in Stabilizers

So far we have considered only discretionary fiscal action. The authorities foresee, or become aware of, some malfunctioning of the economy and, sooner or later, take compensatory action of a type, and on a scale which they consider practicable, to correct it. There are difficulties about timing such action.

A. W. Phillips has exposed some general difficulties after a careful study of dynamic models. He has shown that lags in applying corrective measures could make things worse instead of better. One obvious case occurs if action to correct an upswing is so delayed as not to bite until recession has already begun, and so aggravates the downswing; but there can also be similar trouble with less extreme delays. Obviously a policy based on proper forecasts of the economic situation is likely to do better on this count than one which follows behind events. Another finding is very important:

If the lags in the real economic system are at all similar to those we have used in the models it is unlikely that the period needed to restore any desired equilibrium conditions after an economy has experienced a severe disturbance could be much less than two years, even assuming that the regulating authorities use the policy which is most appropriate to the real system of relationships existing in the economy. As these relationships are not known quantitatively, it is unlikely that the policy applied will be the most appropriate one; it may well cause cyclical fluctuations rather than eliminate them.[1]

It has long been recognized that there are other difficulties in functional finance. Current government spending on goods

[1] A. W. Phillips, *Economic Journal*, 1957, p. 276.

and services is largely connected with the protective and administrative functions of the state, and should not, therefore, be made subject to large or sudden changes. Interest payments cannot be suddenly adjusted without destroying public credit, and few would think it desirable to vary social security payments independently of the need for such provision. There is, however, one class of benefits which should and does vary contracyclically; unemployment benefits automatically increase during a recession and decrease during a boom, thereby steadying aggregate demand.

Public works are more easily varied than current expenditures, although earlier Keynesians exaggerated their flexibility. The Swedes long ago saw that, when a recession threatens, it takes considerable time to make adequate technical preparations for complex or expensive schemes. But only recently has a conflict between stability and growth become apparent in this connection. When inflation develops, public works should be cut down to offset it, but the possibilities of cutting may seem quite limited. In a growing or developing economy there are usually large needs for investment, public as well as private, and if public investment is checked development will be threatened, or social problems will arise, through lags in roading, communications, housing and schools. Recent stress on economic growth has thus tended to favour the idea that government capital formation should be geared to long-term needs for development, rather than exposed to sudden alterations in order to offset business cycles.

Emphasis has thus shifted to taxation as the best fiscal weapon for controlling aggregate demand. It is here, too, that we find the strongest fiscal tendency for an automatic stabilization of aggregate demand. Collections, both of direct and indirect taxes, varying as they do with incomes and sales, must, if rates are steady, increase during a boom and decrease during a recession. Disposable private income, accordingly, changes in smaller proportion than national income and, to that extent, acts as a 'ratchet' against movements in private spending.

Proposals have thus been made for strengthening such automatic correctives by 'built-in stabilizers'. The private but influential American Committee on Economic Development published, in 1947, a plan along those lines. Both current and capital government expenditures should be determined on the basis of social needs and so kept on something like a stable trend. Tax rates should be so fixed as to yield a modest surplus at full employment (96 per cent) of the labour force. As employment fell below this level the surplus would give place to a deficit, and the deficit would check the decline of aggregate demand.

Milton Friedman, soon after, published a wider plan which incorporated an automatic monetary policy along with the automatic fiscal policy. The four main elements of his proposals were:

(a) A double reform of the banking system to eliminate both credit creation by commercial banks and any discretionary control over the volume of money by the central bank. Private creation is best eliminated by adopting the plan for 100 per cent money, which would require full cash reserves against cheque deposits. Discretionary power would be removed from the central bank by abolishing open market operations and thus limiting its functions to mechanical creation or retirement of money in accordance with government deficits or surpluses.

(b) The volume of both government consumption and capital formation to be fixed, and varied, entirely on the basis of the community's long-term desire and willingness to pay for them.

(c) A predetermined programme of transfer expenditures fixing basic rates for social security benefits; absolute outlays on unemployment benefits would automatically vary in a stabilizing way.

(d) Taxation to be largely, if not entirely, based upon a progressive personal income tax, promptly collected at source. Rates and exemptions would be fixed according to that level of income which corresponds to reasonably full employment at a predetermined price level. This hypothetical tax yield might provide for a balanced budget at the full employment level of income, or for a deficit which would provide for a specified secular increase in the volume of money.

The essence of this fourfold proposal is that it uses automatic adaptations in the government contribution to the current income stream to offset, at least in part, changes in other segments of aggregate demand and to change appropriately the supply of money. It eliminates discretionary action in response to cyclical movements as well as some extraneous or perverse reactions of our present monetary and fiscal structure. Discretionary action is limited to determining the hypothetical level of income underlying the stable budget. . . . government expenditures would be financed by either tax revenues or the creation of money. . . . Deficits or surpluses . . . would be reflected dollar for dollar in changes in the quantity of money . . . (and) themselves become automatic consequences of changes in the level of business activity.

Friedman,[1] however, also emphasizes the modesty of his proposal.

It does not claim to provide full employment in the absence of successful measures to make prices of finished goods and of factors of production flexible. It does not claim to eliminate entirely cyclical fluctuations of output and employment. Its claim to serious consideration is that it provides a stable framework of fiscal and monetary action, that it largely eliminates the uncertainty and undersirable politcal consequences of discretionary action . . . (and) that it provides for adaption of the government sector to changes occurring in other sectors of the economy of a kind designed to offset the effect of these changes.

Ackley has emphasized that, under current conditions, built-in stabilizers have a strong effect; he says that they reduce any change of disposable personal income in the United States to about one-half of a corresponding change in GNP.[2] Few economists, however, believe that stabilizers can be built into the economy to such an extent as to avoid all need for discretionary action. Such action, of course, becomes easier as the need for it lessens, and the greater stability of most economies

---

[1] A Monetary and Fiscal Framework for Economic Stability, *American Economic Review*, 1948.

[2] G. Ackley, *Macroeconomics*, p. 302.

since 1946 may well have resulted from more or less planned extensions of such built-in stabilizers as social welfare benefits and income taxes. There still, however, seems need for deliberate action to cope with sudden emergencies, especially over the balance of payments.

13.5 Fiscal Policy and Demand Inflation

By considering a single target of full employment, we have discussed mainly conditions of depression or deficient aggregate demand. The more common postwar situation has been the problem of controlling inflation. There are, however, two conditions under which fiscal action may achieve the double target of a high level of employment and stability of prices. One occurs if changes in prices depend upon excess demand for goods; the other if prices depend upon wages and money wages themselves upon excess demand for labour. These conditions may be thought of most naturally in connection with Klein's version of the classical model, where interest has no effect upon aggregate demand. Then, as we saw, there would not be enough equations in the classical model to determine prices, wages and interest.

We may, accordingly, add an equation which relates prices, in some way, to aggregate demand. One view about prices is that they are directly determined by demand conditions in the goods market. This could mean, supposing, with such quantity theorists as Patinkin, that changes in the price of goods depend upon the excess of aggregate demand over output, and so adding the equation

$$\Delta P = Y - Z.$$

The goods market would then determine both output and prices so that if fiscal policy succeeded both in bringing aggregate demand up to the level required for full employment, and in preventing it from rising above this level, it would have achieved the double target of full employment of labour and stability of prices. Interest would be determined by the money market, and money wages by the labour market.

Another view, however, is that prices, so far from being directly related to demand for goods, are adjusted to costs, and these depend mainly upon money wage rates as the largest influence on unit labour costs. But if money wage rates themselves depend upon the demand for labour we have, in the end, prices also being determined by demand conditions. The missing equations would be:

$$P = aw$$
$$\Delta w = \beta(N - \gamma N^f),$$

showing that prices are proportional to wages, and the change of wages proportional to excess demand for labour above some proportion of full employment. The goods market then determines output and the demand for labour, the labour market determines money wages and prices, and the money market again determines interest.

Fiscal policy could thus ensure stability of prices by preventing demand for goods from rising so high as to cause excess demand for labour. But this may be possible only by modifying the target for employment. Phillips has argued that, for the United Kingdom from 1860, and for Australia from 1949, money wages are not stable at full employment levels.[1] The bargaining position of labour becomes so strong if there is no unemployment that money wages are pushed up, with consequent inflation of prices. He has, however, also argued that changes in wages are closely related to unemployment, so that a sufficient degree of unemployment would make for stability of wages and prices. In the United Kingdom he puts this at 5 per cent ($\gamma = \cdot 95$), and in Australia at $2\frac{1}{2}$ per cent ($\gamma = \cdot 975$). If these figures are accepted, then fiscal policy could be applied so as to achieve price stability only if employment is something less than full.

If this modification of the full employment target is not acceptable, or if the conditions under which fiscal policy can achieve the double target do not hold, then we have to look to a second instrument for achieving price stability, and discuss this in Chapter 15.

[1] *Economica*, 1958.

CHAPTER 14

Monetary Policy

14.1 Monetary Instruments

Monetary policy, we have seen, is best regarded as regulation of credit conditions by the government or central bank. Its importance depends upon the extent to which credit conditions, in turn, influence private spending and there has been much debate about that. Before, however, considering the major issues it is as well to remind ourselves of the main types of monetary instrument.

The oldest instrument, and perhaps the most important for Western Europe, is *discount rate* and associated eligibility requirements. The central bank, by fixing the rate and terms for its own loans to commercial banks and other financial intermediaries, exerts an immediate, and often dominant, influence upon short-term rates of interest and also, perhaps, upon business expectations. Discount rate remains of great importance in regulating international movements of short-term capital between financial centres, but its more direct influence upon domestic conditions has severely waned with the dwindling of commercial bills, the rise of tax rates, the growth of self-finance and spread of nationalized industries.

In the United States, the Federal Reserve Board regards *open market operations* in government securities (and bankers' acceptances) as its major instrument. They are also important in the United Kingdom and Canada but, in many countries, are limited by legislation which restricts central bank holdings of, or dealings in, government securities and, in others, are not practicable on a large enough scale because of small or narrow capital markets.

For such countries the main method has become variation of *reserve requirements* which fix the deposits which commercial banks are obliged to lodge with the central bank. Although the United States was the first country to adopt this method of regulation, the Federal Reserve Board had used it rather infrequently and only for effecting major changes in credit.

Money markets are affected, both directly and indirectly, by government *debt management* which, if not determined, nor always carried out, by the central bank, usually involves some co-operation with it. Debt management has two aspects. Expansion or retirement of issues affects the size of the debt, and public holdings of government bonds may be regarded as an aspect of liquidity. Refunding operations adjust the maturity composition of debt, and so the time spread of liquidity.

There are also a variety of selective and *direct controls*, such as controls over stock market or real estate credit in order to check 'speculation', regulation of hire purchase credit, screening bank loans over a certain minimum size or for different purposes, import pre-deposit requirements to regulate external payments, and differential discount rates, eligibility requirements or reserve requirements applied discriminatorily by the central bank to commercial banks. Such controls were important under wartime inflation, and were retained by many countries for some years later, but they have such serious weaknesses that their use greatly declined as central banks were allowed to apply more general instruments.

14.2   Money, Interest and Spending

The classical idea is that monetary policy acts upon private spending through the rate of interest. In the long-run, it was held, interest is a real phenomenon, determined by the goods market at a level that balances saving and investment. But, in the short-run, the quantity of money does influence market rates of interest so that monetary policy should be used in order to expedite adjustment towards a new equilibrium, and so to lessen unemployment or to check inflation. At the same time, such a policy assists price stability. As we have seen, this approach dates back to Ricardo, if not to Henry Thornton, but seems also to be reflected in recent statements of the Federal Reserve Board.[1]

The argument is attractive, but has difficulties. The first relates to the rather loose connection between the short-term rates that are most immediately affected by monetary changes, and the long-term rates that are more likely to influence private spending. In the United Kingdom the Bank of England has traditionally operated by adjusting discount rate, ensuring a similar adjustment of short-rates by dealings in Government shorts. In the United States the Federal Reserve Board has sought to control short-rates by open market operations, adjustments of discount rate then usually following the market changes. Some authorities think there is sufficient competition and cross-dealing between various financial markets to give short-rates a reasonably prompt and appreciable influence upon long-rates. Thus J. Culbertson has found that, in the United States, short- and long-rates have moved together even if there was much more variation in short-rates.[2] In the United Kingdom, however, the relation has been far from close; according to Hawtrey[3] Bank Rate seldom altered the yield on Consols by more than $\frac{1}{8}$ per cent, and the Radcliffe Report also finds a weak connection for the 1950's.[4]

This weakness might well be remedied, as Keynes[5] suggested it should be:

Perhaps a complex offer by the central bank to buy and sell at stated prices gilt-edged bonds of all maturities, in place of a single bank rate for short-term bills, is the most important practical improvement which can be made in the technique of monetary management.

The advice, of course, was being tendered to the Bank of England. In terms of American practice it would mean open

[1] e.g. Influence of Credit and Monetary Measures on Economic Stability, *Federal Reserve Bulletin*, March, 1953.

[2] *Quarterly Journal of Economics*, 197.

[3] R. G. Hawtrey, *A Century of Bank Rate*, p. 170.

[4] Op. cit., pp. 155-7.

[5] J. M. Keynes, *The General Theory of Employment, Interest and Money*, p. 206.

market operations in mediums or longs as well as in shorts, and during 1961 the Federal Reserve Board, after much urging from various critics, began to experiment along these lines.

The second difficulty has been noted earlier – empirical, more especially econometric, evidence suggests that interest changes have little influence upon the mass of investment or consumption. Hawtrey persistently argued that short-term rates governed investment in non-perishable inventories, and that this was the traditional view about the working of Bank Rate. Critics, from Tooke to Keynes, rejected it by pointing to the small weight of interest in relation to carrying costs or price uncertainties, and they have been supported by such econometricians as Tinbergen. Both Hawtrey and Keynes agreed, at one time, that interest could have little effect upon investment in manufacturing equipment because of uncertainties about prices, operating costs and proper obsolescence allowances. Keynes did hold that interest could have a marked effect upon investment in building, transport and public utilities, and econometric studies give some support to this view, but not for thinking that interest has an appreciable effect upon aggregate investment. The econometricians are supported here by the *Radcliffe Report*[1]:

> The insignificance of interest changes in relation to other costs and to the risks involved was emphasized to us again and again, in relation not only to fixed investment but also to stocks of commodities.

14.3 Monetary Policy and Liquidity

Patinkin, as we saw, holds that, even if aggregate demand is not influenced by interest, it is nevertheless influenced by liquidity so that monetary policy could control spending more directly than the classical view envisaged. A fall of aggregate demand, for example, below full employment level would, in time, be remedied by a fall of prices which increased real money balances and so aggregate demand. Such an adjustment may be long or painful, but could be eased if the central bank promptly increased the supply of money to raise liquidity.

[1] Op. cit., p. 158.

This argument depends upon the reality and strength of the *direct* influence of real money balances upon demand. There appears to be more convincing evidence for this real balance effect than for an interest effect, but it is perhaps too minor for much reliance to be placed upon monetary policy as a means of stabilizing the economy.

There is, however, another important line of argument which stresses an *indirect* influence of liquidity upon business investment through the supply of loans rather than through the demand for them. It was first advanced by Rosa,[1] taken up in part by the Federal Reserve Board,[2] and more recently by the *Radcliffe Report*.[3]

These authorities all use liquidity in a wider sense than we have so far used it, emphasizing the role of other financial intermediaries than the commercial banks. By liquidity they mean the whole structure of financial assets ranging through money holdings, bills or shorts, equities and all kinds of loans. It is thought that some kind of balance between such assets – a liquidity structure – is kept by financial intermediaries which include, not only commercial banks but also discount, acceptance and issue houses, hire purchase financiers, insurance offices, superannuation or pension funds, investment trusts, building societies, loan associations and savings banks.

The theory has a number of strands but might be roughly summarized along these lines:

(i) Open market sales by the central bank reduce the cash of the institutions which have bought its bills. If the central bank takes no steps to replenish this cash the price of bills will drop, or the short-rate rises. A rise in the short-rate might, of course, be obtained in some countries without open market sales simply by raising Bank Rate.

(ii) The rise in the short-rate has a much greater effect in

[1] R. V. Rosa, 'Interest Rates and the Central Bank', in *Money, Trade and Economic Growth, Essays in Honor of John Henry Williams*, (1951).
[2] *Federal Reserve Bulletin*, March 1953, pp. 3–6.
[3] Op. cit., Ch. VI.

reducing liquidity than the reduction of money in circulation through open market sales. *All* financial intermediaries, and other businesses holding shorts, find their liquidity position impaired through the fall in the market price of bills. That in itself may check spending by nonfinancial businesses, and should force financial intermediaries to make some adjustments. They may seek to restore liquidity by building up larger cash reserves out of funds flowing to them from depositors or savers; if so, their purchases of bills and bonds, or their new loans to business borrowers, must correspondingly decline. The process may well be accentuated by uncertainty over the future short-rate, and the central bank can always act so as to foster such uncertainty.

(iii) Financial intermediaries, alternatively, may seek to restore liquidity by selling bonds, so that the long-rate also rises. The central bank could hasten such a fall by including bonds as well as bills in open market sales, or by using its control over public debt management for the same purpose.

(iv) The rise in the long-rate, depressing bond values, further impairs the liquidity of businesses holding bonds. That may also check some spending by ordinary business firms. Financial intermediaries have to make another adjustment to their liquidity structure and, again, may increase their cash balances, or else their bill holdings, at the expense of lending operations. New loans are especially likely to be restricted if rates of interest charged for them are hard to adjust quickly, because there will then be less conflict for financial intermediaries between liquidity and profitability.

(v) The capital market, as a whole, is far from perfect in the sense that demands for finance are promptly adjusted to the supply by interest changes. Lenders, moreover, have other requirements besides interest payments, e.g. collateral, period and amortization. Borrowers are thus willing to take more at any rate charged than lenders will grant so that, in Keynes's classic phrase, there is normally 'a fringe of unsatisfied borrowers'.[1] When, because of the preceding impairment of liquidity, lenders find adjustments necessary, they are likely to ration credit more severely.

(vi) Business investment, as well as residential construction and consumer credit, is, to a considerable extent, financed by loans from financial intermediaries. These important types of private spending are thus likely to be checked by central banking action to reduce the supply of money and to raise interest rates. There has, it is true, been a marked secular growth of internal financing from retained profits (particularly among manufacturing companies), and this tends to insulate business from credit rationing. But a good deal of finance is also raised through public issues, and these have come to depend partly upon subscriptions of financial intermediaries as they have sought a hedge against inflation by switching from bonds to equities.

The theory is impressive. It is based upon a sophisticated knowledge of money markets and, by emphasizing the effect of interest upon liquidity and of liquidity upon lending, avoids the difficulties of older views that interest strongly influences the investors who borrow funds. There are, nevertheless, difficulties in accepting it.

The crux of the theory, however softly it is put, is that financial intermediaries have sufficiently rigid ideas about their liquidity structure; as cash is depleted or interest rates rise, they will, sooner or later, cut down ordinary lending. But interest rates rise with boom conditions, or as a result of central banking action to restrain such conditions, and in a boom there is both an increasing demand for loans and an apparent improvement, through rising sales and profits, in the credit-worthiness of most borrowers. Both the profitability and apparent safety of lending to business may improve so much as to make financial intermediaries relax ideas about a suitable

[1] *A Treatise on Money*, Vol. II, p. 364.

liquidity structure of their assets. Something like this happened in the United States during the boom of 1954–7 when, in spite of strong attempts by the Federal Reserve Board to make the Rosa doctrine work, commercial banks, among other financial intermediaries, went on selling bonds at worsening prices in order to expand more profitable loans to customers.

The difficulty might be met, at least in part, as Gurley and Shaw have suggested,[1] by extending central bank control from commercial banks to non-bank lenders by imposing liquidity rules upon them also. Sayers says 'the Radcliffe Committee looked at the question and shuddered'.[2] Their reason for shuddering was 'not mainly because of its administrative burdens, but also because the further growth of new financial institutions would allow the situation continually to slip from under the grip of the authorities'.[3] On this view, then, for better or for worse, the possibilities of monetary control rest largely upon vigorous adjustment of interest rates. But even Sayers lacks faith in that; 'lest this should (as I suspect) prove a non-starter we must think again on how the flexibility of fiscal policy might be improved'.

There is a further limitation in that any effects upon the liquidity of financial intermediaries achieved by such a policy are likely to have only temporary or once-over effects upon investment or aggregate demand. For if the liquidity of financial intermediaries is reduced, and they are forced to restore the position by curtailing new loans, investment will also be curtailed to the limited extent that it depends upon new loans from such intermediaries. But once they have adjusted their liquidity position, financial intermediaries can continue new lending on the old scale, so that any setback they give to investment need be only transient.

In case this discussion appears to show inadequate faith in central banks it may be as well to indicate the more optimistic

[1] J. G. Gurley and E. S. Shaw, *Financial Aspects of Economic Development*, Journal of Finance, 1956.

[2] *Economic Journal*, 1960, p. 722.

[3] *Report of Committee on the Working of the Monetary System*, Cmnd. 827, p. 134.

views of the U.S. *Commission on Money and Credit* whose report was published in 1961. Key quotations are given without explicit comment.

(1) Monetary restraint causes a reduction in the willingness and ability of nearly all institutional lenders to meet the expanding credit demand. While it is difficult to make any precise assessment of the volume of loans refused or reduced during recent tight money episodes, it appears to have been substantial. (p. 50).

(2) Unfortunately studies of the actual behaviour of business investment and interest rate have not reliably isolated the effect of monetary policy from shifts in other determinants of investment. Fragmentary evidence, however, indicates that some kinds of investment are sensitive to changes in interest costs. . . . The evidence indicates that changes in credit have some, but only a slight, effect on consumer expenditures for other than residential construction. (p. 52).

(3) While the processes and channels through which monetary measures operate are the same for a policy of ease as for a policy of restriction, an expansionist policy may be less effective than a restrictive policy. (p. 54).

(4) The Commission believes that the restrictive monetary policies in 1955–57 and again in 1959 demonstrate that monetary policy can have a very substantial effect on the level and rate of growth of demand. In both periods monetary restriction seemed to induce a decline in the annual rate of residential construction of $3 to $4 billion. Business investment was lower than it would have been if credit had been available at low rates. (p. 55).

(5) The average rate of growth of the money supply should reflect the rate of growth of real output at high employment and stable prices. However, the exact rate of growth of money supply will have to depend on the strength of private demand and the character of fiscal policy in that these will affect the demand for money. (p. 61).

CHAPTER 15

Income Policy

15.1 Wages Policy and Full Employment

A classical prescription for full employment was reduction of the real wage rate. It was based on the idea that, in the full classical model set out earlier, unemployment could arise only from some lack of balance between the demand for labour and the supply. In time, of course, an excess supply of labour would be removed by market forces pushing down the real wage, but this might well be a slow and painful process which could be speeded up if workers accepted a cut of real wages.

This prescription depends upon the supply of labour rising as the real wage increases. If, however, we have the supply of labour infinitely elastic at the ruling wage rate, then a very large reduction of this real wage rate might be needed to secure

full employment, e.g. from $\left(\dfrac{w}{p}\right)_1$ to $\left(\dfrac{w}{p}\right)_2$ in the opposite diagram.

So large a reduction might be impossible to achieve in practice.

It also depends upon the assumption that prices are determined by demand conditions and hence unaffected by the wage cut except in so far as this reacted indirectly upon aggregate demand for goods. For wages policy or wage bargaining can fix only the *money* wage rate, and a reduction of this means a fall of the real wage rate only if prices are not thereby affected.

Keynes tended to take the different view that prices are

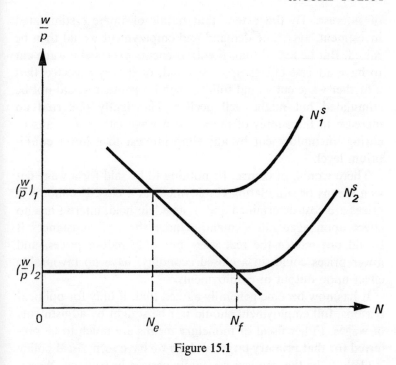

Figure 15.1

cost-determined, and largely dependent upon money wage rates. If so, a cut in money wages would leave real wages, and hence unemployment, unaffected.

> There may exist no expedient by which labour as a whole can reduce its *real* wage to a given figure by making revised *money* bargains with the entrepreneurs.[1]

He did admit that, in an open economy, a wage cut, by reducing prices, would encourage exports and discourage imports, thus increasing aggregate demand and employment.[2] He also pointed out that the price reductions following a cut of wages would increase the real value of money balances, and lower the rate

[1] *The General Theory*, p. 13.
[2] Op. cit., p. 262.

of interest. To the extent that a fall of interest stimulated investment, aggregate demand and employment would then be raised. But he feared that, if entrepreneurs expected a wage cut to have adverse effects upon demand, or if they expected that a further wage cut would follow, then investment would not be stimulated but might well decline. He rightly preferred an increase in the supply of money to a wage cut as a means of curing unemployment by adjusting interest to a lower equilibrium level.

There would, of course, be nothing to be said for a wage cut as a means of stimulating employment in a closed economy if prices are cost-determined and if, as Klein held, interest has no effect upon aggregate demand. Under these circumstances it would not reduce the real wage but only reduce prices, and lower prices could, in a closed economy, have no favourable effect upon output or employment.

It has now become generally agreed that, if only for political reasons, full employment should not be sought by adjustments of wages. Either fiscal or monetary means are much to be preferred for that primary target and, as we have seen, fiscal policy is likely to be the stronger and more certain instrument. Wages policy has thus become advocated as a means of achieving some other target and, most commonly, as a means of controlling price inflation.

The possibility, however, of using controls over wages, *if these can be applied*, obviously depends upon the extent to which prices are cost-determined and upon the extent to which wages are influenced by other factors than demand for labour. This is an empirical question, but the evidence is still not clear.

15.2 Cost-push versus Demand-pull Inflation

The great inflations of the past were associated with wars. Large increases of government spending, accompanied by large increases in the supply of money, led to a general shortage of consumer goods and to a rise in their prices. From consumers' markets the pressure spread to other markets. Unemployment diminished in the process, as labour became scarce, too. All this is illustrated by the following table:

Table 15.1 Prices, Money and Unemployment during Inflationary Periods in the United States

Period	Consumer Prices[1]	Money[2]	Unemployment Rate[1]
			p.c.
1914–19	42·9– 74·0	20·0– 35·6	8·0–2·3
1939–44	59·4– 75·2	60·9–136·2	17·2–1·2
1950–52	102·8–113·5	173·8–191·0	5·0–2·7

[1] Source: Joint Economic Committee, *Productivity, Prices and Income*, 1957.
[2] Source: L. R. Klein and R. F. Kosobud, *Quarterly Journal of Economics*, May, 1961.

After 1955, however, there was the rather novel development of prices rising while unemployment was increasing and the supply of money was slowing down.

Table 15.2 Prices, Money and Unemployment, 1955-9, in the United States

Year	Consumer Prices	Money	Unemployment Rate
		$b.	p.c.
1955	114·5	216·6	4·4
1956	116·2	222·0	4·2
1957	120·2	227·7	4·3
1958	123·5	242·6	6·8
1959	124·5	246·3	5·5

Source: President's *Economic Report*, 1960.

Nor was this phenomenon limited to the United States. The United Nations' *World Economic Survey for 1957* pointed to a new 'creeping inflation' that affected the industrial countries after 1953. It was called 'creeping' because price increases, although persistent, were much more modest than in previous inflations and, for the first time, were not generated by abnormal forces of war or of post-war readjustment but were associated with normal forces of economic growth. It continued, moreover, after the onset of recession in mid-1957. In the United Kingdom, for example, prices continued rising during 1957 and 1958,

171

although employment fell; this was also true for Sweden, the Netherlands, France and Canada among other countries.

A vigorous discussion arose about the causes of such inflation and the way to remedy it. To some it seemed that so long as prices were rising there must be excess demand pressures, and that monetary or fiscal restraints could check both. To others it seemed that such restraints would not hold down prices but would rather increase unemployment. The latter group believed that prices are 'administered', i.e. fixed by sellers on a cost-plus basis, but from this point they split.

Businessmen tended to blame unions for pushing up wages, or at least for increases above the growth of labour productivity. In the postwar situations of near full employment, and with governments committed to avoiding serious unemployment, unions could push for higher wages fairly vigorously. The first round of any wage increase might occur in dynamic industries where labour productivity was rapidly advancing. Success for labour in these favoured industries might not push up prices, but other unions would follow suit and spread cumulative wage increase across a wide range of industries, in many of which growth of labour productivity would be well below that of the leaders.

Trade unionists, naturally, resisted this interpretation of rising prices as their responsibility. They argued, instead, that the main cause of price increases was a rise of profit margins in oligopolistic industries. The explanation of how oligopolists were able to do this profitably during a period of sagging general demand was that they had a reserve of unexploited monopoly power; i.e. they had not been as ruthlessly profit-seeking as they could have been in a previous period. Senator O'Mahoney, influenced by this line of thought, introduced a bill in 1958, the preamble of which stated: 'inflation will be checked if the pricing policies of . . . corporations are publicly reviewed before increased prices may be made effective'. Price control, of some kind, that is, should be applied not only in wartime conditions of excess demand but in peacetime conditions of creeping, cost-push inflation.

On the other side of the whole controversy are those who deny that there can be any such thing as cost-push inflation, on the ground that cost increases can be passed on to prices only if aggregate demand increases rapidly enough to absorb output at the higher prices. Otherwise there will be downward pressure upon profit margins from excess supply, and downward pressure upon wages through growing unemployment.

Phillips,[1] in a pioneer article, made a statistical analysis of British wages, 1861–1957, which seemed to show that these had been largely determined by excess demand for labour, as indicated by the increase in the percentage of workers unemployed, and concluded that price stability required a rate of unemployment around 5 per cent. His equation was:

$$\frac{\Delta w}{w} = -0{\cdot}9 + 9{\cdot}638u^{-1{\cdot}394}.$$

Wages, and hence prices, seemed to be largely determined by excess demand for labour which, itself, would depend upon the aggregate demand for goods.

But his analysis was rather rough, and so defective. His associate Lipsey[2] reworked the problem using better statistical methods to obtain;

$$\frac{\Delta w}{w} = -1{\cdot}21 + 6{\cdot}45u^{-1} + 2{\cdot}26u^{-2} - 0{\cdot}19\left(\frac{\Delta u}{u}\right) + {\cdot}21\left(\frac{\Delta p}{p}\right)$$
$$(2{\cdot}12) \quad (2{\cdot}13) \quad (0{\cdot}004) \quad ({\cdot}07)$$

for the period 1862–1913, and

$$\frac{\Delta w}{w} = 0{\cdot}74 + 0{\cdot}43u^{-1} + 11{\cdot}18u^{-4} + 0{\cdot}038\left(\frac{\Delta u}{u}\right) + 0{\cdot}69\left(\frac{\Delta p}{p}\right)$$
$$(2{\cdot}10) \quad (6{\cdot}00) \quad (0{\cdot}012) \quad (0{\cdot}08)$$

for the period 1923–39 and 1948–57. Lipsey comments that, although these results suggest wage-rates were largely demand-determined before 1913, after that a cost-push influence entered

[1] A. W. Phillips, *Economica*, Nov. 1958.
[2] R. G. Lipsey, *Economica*, February 1960.

more strongly, as indicated by the rise in the parameter for the rate of change of prices.

The analysis so far conducted is . . . not inconsistent with the hypothesis that there is a strong feed-back from price changes to wage changes with a great deal—but not all of the rise in wages being attributed to wages chasing prices.

Dicks-Mireaux and Dow[1] attempted a similar analysis of British wages for the period 1946–56 using a special index, H, of excess demand for labour constructed from data for vacancies as well as for unemployment. Their equation was

$$\frac{\Delta w}{w} = 0 \cdot 11 + 0 \cdot 52 \left(\frac{\Delta p}{p}\right) + 3 \cdot 64H$$
$$(0 \cdot 05) \qquad (0 \cdot 40)$$

Here both prices and excess demand for labour appeared to have considerable influence on wage changes, but that demand was much the stronger.

All these investigators took a single equation, but it would obviously be better to use a simultaneous equation method of estimation based on some plausible model. This has been attempted by Hines[2] with the following results, for British data, 1921–38 and 1948–61;

$$\Delta w = -1 \cdot 9740 + 1 \cdot 5945 \Delta z + 0 \cdot 1282z + 0 \cdot 6804 \Delta P - 0 \cdot 0812 \Delta P_{-1}$$
$$(0 \cdot 2418) \quad (0 \cdot 0409) \quad (0 \cdot 1129) \quad (0 \cdot 0276)$$

$$-0 \cdot 0441u$$
$$(0 \cdot 0370)$$

$$\Delta p = -0 \cdot 7797 + 0 \cdot 6924 \Delta w + 0 \cdot 03396 \Delta P_{m-\frac{1}{2}} + 0 \cdot 1346 \Delta q$$
$$(0 \cdot 0348) \quad (0 \cdot 0173) \quad (0 \cdot 0725)$$

$$\Delta T = 1 \cdot 4014 - 0 \cdot 1145 T_{-1} + 0 \cdot 4664 \Delta P - 0 \cdot 0987 \Delta P + 0 \cdot 0149 R_{-\frac{1}{2}}$$
$$(0 \cdot 0083) \quad (0 \cdot 0148) \quad (0 \cdot 0129) \quad (0 \cdot 0048)$$

where z denotes percentage of the labour force unionized, q industrial production per worker, P_m import prices and R profits (amount).

Hines interprets his results as showing an influence of unionization on wage changes as well as an influence from the cost of

[1] *Journal of Royal Statistical Society*, Part II, 1959.
[2] A. G. Hines, *Review of Economic Studies*, Oct. 1964.

174

living. A 10 per cent rise of prices would tend to raise wages by nearly 7 per cent; but wages also affect prices as a 10 per cent increase of British wages similarly tended to raise prices by nearly 7 per cent. But Hines considered that 'the level of unemployment does not appear to be an important factor in the determination of the rate of change of wage rates of the sample period,' – an opposite conclusion to that of Phillips. These results – unionization depending upon prices, wages upon both, and prices upon wages – are far more suggestive of cost-push inflation than of demand inflation.

Eckstein and Wilson,[1] however, seem to reach an opposite result for the United States in an analysis of the period 1948–60. They found, for industries which played a key role in setting wage increase, a relation

$$\Delta w = -5\cdot74 + 0\cdot73R - 0\cdot56u$$
$$(0\cdot04) \quad (0\cdot06)$$

which suggests that profit rates, R, had a stronger influence than unemployment upon money wage rates, and both of these explanatory variables are related to demand conditions. Klein and Goldberger, on the other hand, have a wage adjustment equation for the United States,

$$w_\theta - w_{\theta-1} = 4\cdot11 - 0\cdot75u_\theta + 0\cdot56\,(P_{\theta-1} - P_{\theta-2}) + 0\cdot56\,(\theta - 1929)$$
$$(0\cdot63) \quad (0\cdot30) \qquad\qquad (0\cdot20)$$

which gives a marked influence of prices upon wages, although none of their coefficients are at all reliable.

More recent work by Sargan[2] on British data throws doubt on the hypothesis that wages tend to be adjusted to the cost of living. One of his equations, expressed in logarithmic values and using quarterly data, is

$$\frac{w_\theta}{w_{\theta-1}} = 0\cdot0120 U_{\theta-1} + \cdot00133\theta - 0\cdot271 \left(\frac{w}{p}\right)_{\theta-1}$$
$$(\cdot0058) \qquad\quad (\cdot00036) \qquad (\cdot073)$$

[1] O. Eckstein and T. A. Wilson, *Quarterly Journal of Economics*, August, 1962. See also *Review of Economic Studies*, April 1968.

[2] J. D. Sargan, 'Wages and Prices in the United Kingdom: a Study in Econometric Methodology', in *Econometric Analysis and National Economic Planning*, (1964).

and may be interpreted in the following way. If there were moving equilibrium, (such that $w_\theta = w_{\theta-1}$), then real wages would rise by about 2 per cent a year, given a constant degree of unemployment, but if unemployment doubled the equilibrium real wage would fall by about 3 per cent. Unions may thus be supposed to seek a 'normal' real wage rate that rises by about 2 per cent a year, but settle for less when unemployment increases. They would, however, try to make good such a deficiency as soon as employment rose again.

Sargan also gives a price-adjustment equation which makes the ratio of prices to wages depend upon the ratio of import prices to wages and upon three other influences for which estimates of coefficients are unsatisfactory. When this equation is also considered, it appears that prices and money wages would ultimately change in the same proportion as import prices (in domestic currency), a result which implies, for example, that devaluation is, in the end, only inflationary. But there is a long lag of 13 quarters before money wages rise by one-half of the percentage change in import prices, and 43 quarters before money wages achieve 90 per cent of their complete adjustment, and hence a long period during which devaluation can have some effect upon the balance of trade by altering domestic import or export prices.

15.3 Wages Policy in the Netherlands

Tinbergen, until 1956 the Director of the Netherlands Central Planning Bureau, argues strongly that centralized regulation of wages is the best means of promoting price stability. This follows from the view that prices are cost-determined and that the double target of full employment and price stability requires two instruments. Fiscal policy can help to secure full employment, but full employment by no means guarantees price stability, even if excess demand is eliminated. It might be thought that, as there is more than one fiscal instrument, fiscal policy could do both jobs. But the only fiscal instrument which has a direct effect on prices is expenditure taxes, which make for higher prices because they tend to be added to costs. His objection to them as a possible instrument for price stability is that they would have to be sufficiently high 'to allow a reduction of the size needed to counteract an excessive rise, say, in wage rates'. Other alternatives to wage regulations have serious drawbacks. Varying the interest rate is almost useless because interest has little influence on prices. Direct price control requires a complicated administration and leads to socio-economic frictions.

For these reasons, he says,[1] wage rates have to be a deliberate instrument of policy if employment targets and monetary equilibrium (i.e. price stability) are to be pursued at the same time. There is an important and well-known argument against making wage rates an instrument of economic policy. It is felt by many that wages should be a subject for 'free negotiation' between workers' and employers' organisations. Making wages subject to government approval or even decree would be, following this line of thought, a tendency towards totalitarianism. In the author's opinion, the desire for 'freedom' in wage negotiations is very close to an inconsistency. The real freedom, of course, is very small, since the choice of a wage rate deviating from the one required by 'full' employment and monetary equilibrium will endanger one, or both, of these targets. And the assertion regarding totalitarianism seems to be exaggerated respecting countries in which trade unions have an important influence on the decisions taken by the government.

In the Netherlands unions have played a very full role in economic policy. During the war there was clandestine co-operation between workers and employers to ameliorate and frustrate the German occupation and, after the war, the central organizations of employers and the central trade unions created the Foundation of Labour as a permanent instrument for co-operation, aimed at ensuring 'good permanent social relations in Dutch industrial life on a basis of co-operation between employers and workers'. Although an unofficial organization, the Foundation immediately became an advisory body to the Government. In 1950 a Social and Economic Council was created by statute to give advice on economic as well as social

[1] J. Tinbergen, *Economic Policy, Principles and Design*, p. 84.

questions; it has equal representation of workers, employers and independent experts appointed by the Government.

The fixing of wages, however, is in the hands of an official Board of Government Conciliators which has power to 'establish binding rules for, and in relation to, wages and other conditions of employment'. An employer paying higher or lower wages than those fixed by the Board is liable to legal penalties. The Board does not consist of civil servants but of independent men chosen from all parties, and having some personal authority in regard to labour questions. Before reaching any decision, moreover, it is bound to consult the Foundation of Labour.

Wages policy is mainly a result of endless and perpetual negotiations with the organisations of employers and workers both in separate industries and also with them as a totality knitted together in the Foundation of Labour. In very important matters negotiations are conducted between the Minister of Social Affairs or even the Cabinet and the Foundation. In other matters of a general character and on all important questions concerning a single bracket of industry, the decisions are the result of discussions and negotiations between the Board and the Foundation of Labour.[1]

Guiding principles for wage fixing were drawn in agreement with the Foundation. A minimum level of wages was established on the basis of an investigation of the cost of providing for the basic needs of a worker with a wife and two children, and differentials of about 10 per cent were fixed between skilled, semi-skilled and unskilled labour. After immediate post-war wage increases had been granted, it was announced that increases of wages would be permitted only if they were coupled with higher productivity and lower costs of production; this provision, of course, aimed at stimulating production as well as at stabilizing prices. In 1948 subsidies of foodstuffs were removed and workers were compensated by a flat wage increase, as they were also after the devaluation of the guilder in 1949.

A remarkable feature of the policy was agreement of unions to accept a reduction of 5 per cent in real wages in order to help

[1] M. G. Levenbach, *Modern Law Review*, October, 1953.

meet the balance of payments crisis which followed the out-
break of the Korean War. The Social and Economic Council
estimated that real consumption should fall by 5 per cent, and
recommended that remaining subsidies should be so cut as to
raise the cost of living by 10 per cent. The Board of Conciliators,
in agreement with the Foundation, granted only a 5 per cent
wage increase, and the resulting fall of real wages did play a
part in overcoming the crisis.

Levenbach lists the results of this policy as follows:

(a) Wages and prices have not played leap-frog, as they have in
other countries.

(b) Wages and prices were kept in hand. Wages have risen in
accordance with a slowly rising curve of increasing real income,
which corresponded with the possibilities of our post-war recon-
struction and recovery.

(c) The wages policy has fostered social justice in several respects
. . . It has improved the relative position of backward groups. It has
eliminated many differences which were unjustified.

(d) The wages policy also aims at an increase in the productivity
of labour . . . by a systematic study and application of scientifically
measured and socially controlled methods such as work classification
and the like.

(e) The need for the system has been widely recognised by
employers' and workers' organisations . . . The self-restraint and
discipline shown by the workers' organisations and their members
are very remarkable. As a result industrial peace has been well
maintained . . . Yet strikes are not forbidden.

A not unsympathetic British observer, however, has expressed
less favourable views.

Neither wage regulation in Holland nor wage restraint in Britain
has been a substitute for a disinflationary financial and budgetary
policy, but it has been a useful supplementary aid to the more
fundamental measures that have been used to check the expansion of
demand . . . The adoption of a centralised system of wage determination is only compatible with free trade unionism and free enterprise
so long as it responds to the economic and political pressures that are

generated in a free society. What is altered when wages are determined by a central body is the manner in which collective bargaining takes place. In the Netherlands, bargaining was not eliminated . . . it was simply transferred from the industrial to the national level . . . Ultimately the outcome of a system of bargaining, whether it be a centralised one like that adopted by the Netherlands, a decentralised one like that of Britain, or an even more decentralised one like that of America, will depend on the power of the contending factions . . . From the evidence examined it would seem fair to conclude that the centralisation of wage determination in the Netherlands has brought some advantages, but that these have not been as great as the supporters of a national wage policy have often claimed. Neither the problem of inflation nor the problem of wage structure has been satisfactorily solved.[1]

The policy was modified in 1959 to widen possibilities of wage differentiation according to sectoral differences in productivity. But the modification was given up in 1961 because a pronounced boom led to great pressure upon wages, and also because the new principle was thought to be theoretically unsound in that above average gains in productivity should lead to corresponding reductions of prices. Further pressures arising from Common Market scarcities of labour badly undermined the whole system late in 1963, and, three years later, an emergency ceiling of 7 per cent had to be put on wage increases.

15.4 Other Attempts

Inflation in the United Kingdom led the government there to similar, if more timid, ideas in the late 1950's. A Council on Prices, Productivity and Incomes was set up to 'report to the nation' about the problem and, in 1961, its recommendation that wages, on the average, should not rise by more than $2\frac{1}{2}$ per cent that year may have had some influence. In the following year, it was replaced by a National Incomes Commission of four appointed members. Parties immediately concerned with any wages claim, including the government, could refer such a claim to the Commission which, after a semi-judicial hearing,

[1] A. C. Roberts, *Economica*, 1957.

would publish its findings and recommendations. The Commission could also recommend fiscal or other government measures for restraining profits. It was handicapped in having no secretariat and also by the hostility of the unions, so that its recommendations were not very effective.

The Labour Government which came to power in 1961 tried to improve such arrangements. A National Board for Prices and Incomes was set up to make recommendations about any relevant matter referred to it by the Government, but there was again no provision for ensuring that these recommendations were put into effect. A subsequent White Paper set out guidelines for prices and incomes, indicating a norm of 3–3½ per cent for average annual increases of money incomes, as that was believed consistent with price stability. In 1965 the National Incomes Commission was dissolved and committees, set up by the C.B.I. and T.U.C., were required to examine notifications of increases in prices or wages and, if they so recommended, these would be referred to the National Board.

In July 1966 heroic measures for strengthening sterling included a six months' freeze of wages, dividends and prices, extended in November to the first half of 1967. Over the whole year of the freeze weekly wage rates and retail prices rose by less than 2½ per cent, about half the previous increase, but much of the slackening came from a general decline of economic activity associated with other measures. A later act enabled the state to delay pay increases for up to seven months pending their consideration by the Prices and Incomes Board, but the main hope of restraint was voluntary co-operation by employers and unions in holding pay increases to 'safe levels'. A *White Paper* of June 1967 redefined these levels as those which were in line with long-term growth of national output and consistent with stability in the general level of prices. More specifically, pay increases should be limited to direct contributions towards higher productivity, to promoting essential changes in the distribution of manpower, to raising depressed wages or salaries to a reasonable level or to correcting glaring disparities in rewards for similar work.

The United States has also been concerned with this problem but has not gone beyond moral suasion. The *Report of the Council of Economic Advisers* for 1962 clarified a number of principles. It favoured, as a non-inflationary norm, a rate of wage increase for *each* industry equal to the *general* trend increase of labour productivity. Wages should be increased to the extent that a sector's gain of productivity exceeded this trend, or reduced by the extent that it fell short. Wage increases, however, could exceed the norm if a sector was short of labour, or reduced below it if labour was redundant. Prices, similarly, could rise in an industry needing more capital than its current profits would attract, or in which other costs than those associated with labour had risen; conversely, prices could fall in an industry suffering from excess capacity. Deviations such as those specified are important because it would be wrong to attempt a freezing of the whole industrial structure. Little reference was made to other types of income than wages in this report.

The *OECD Working Party on Cost of Production and Prices* has published two reports. The first (1962) report quoted the American study approvingly, but could not offer firm advice about qualifications or exceptions to the norm. It stressed the need for public discussion and approval of general principles in keeping money incomes from rising more rapidly than is consistent with price stability. So far, it is only in the Netherlands that individual wage contracts have to be approved within the framework of general norms accepted by government, labour and management. A supplementary report on wage mobility presented statistical findings which threw serious doubt on the idea that differential wage increases were needed for attracting labour to expanding industries. It therefore questioned the practical importance of such deviations from the norm on the ground that labour deployment has been insensitive to changes in relative wages. A similar view was expressed in the *1965 Report of the US Council of Economic Advisers*.

A further OEEC report (1964) dealt with other types of income. It was held that prices might be 'administered' by oligopolistic concerns in such a way as to push them up, although the main reason for controlling profits was to secure the co-operation of labour for wages policy by removing feelings about unfair discrimination. Direct controls over profits are still in an exploratory phase, at least as a permanent policy. They are indirectly controlled in all countries by fiscal or monetary measures, often supplemented by official measures for controlling monopolies or monopolistic practices and, in the case of E.C.E. countries, particularly, by removing barriers to competition through reductions of tariffs or widening customs areas.

Some countries go further, especially Norway and the Netherlands, by using price controls for restraining both wage demands and excessive profits. This has the advantage of acting directly upon prices, stability in which is the aim of incomes policy. But it bristles with difficulties. The general norm is presumably a zero increase, yet there are the same exceptions as those mentioned for wage policy; increase in non-labour costs, need to finance expansion of more rapidly growing industries or need to correct structural imbalances. Another problem is the need to give incentives to management and labour for expansion. The main practical difficulty is that there are widely different changes in productivity which also affect the quality or appearance of products. It is often difficult, in these circumstances, to tell whether a particular price has changed in relation to the accepted norm, and any attempt at keeping them to the norm must require extensive or costly interference with markets.

There is now, accordingly, fairly widespread agreement at governmental levels about the need for an incomes policy. Yet this concensus is in striking contrast to the meagre results so far achieved outside the Netherlands. They may be regarded as the first steps along a difficult road, or as indicating the formidable difficulties in attempting to travel it. This type of policy clearly requires much more than government conviction or willingness to accept responsibility. Far more important is the co-operation of business and labour organizations with the government, and so with each other, in seeking its achievement. Important, but so difficult that one must wish that wages or prices *were* fully determined by demand conditions; for then it would be enough to rely upon fiscal and monetary measures in promoting price stability along with full employment.

CHAPTER 16

Foreign Trade Policy

16.1 The Alternatives

The most troublesome aspect of economic policy, after unemployment, has become the avoidance or correction of unduly large or prolonged deficits in the current balance of external payments. Throughout the post-war era Britain and some other sterling area countries have been plagued with this problem and it has recently bothered even the United States. Twice Britain has tried to meet it by large devaluations of sterling relatively to gold (or the US dollar) and, between 1948 and 1967, by the fiscal-monetary measures disrespectfully labelled 'stop-go' because they have involved alternate damping and stimulation of aggregate demand or economic activity.

Most countries adhere to the International Monetary Fund and its system of stable exchange rates, which allows a variation in a particular rate only to correct a 'fundamental disequilibrium' between the exports and imports of the country concerned. This has meant adhering to fiscal or monetary policies for regulating aggregate demand in order to avoid external deficits at a fixed exchange rate and, at the same time, to maintain something like full employment.

We have seen, in Chapter 7, that imports have a strong tendency to increase with the level of aggregate demand and that exports have a tendency, whose strength depends upon the proportion of home to foreign sale of export goods, to vary in the opposite direction. These connections became stronger under conditions of full employment; for if resources are really fully employed, and if there is no technical progress, then any increase of aggregate demand would have to be absorbed by an

185

increase of imports plus a decrease of exports as more export goods were diverted to the home market.

It is, accordingly, very important that fiscal and monetary measures prevent excess demands for goods or services under conditions approaching full employment, especially in a country which has no abundance of foreign exchange reserves. These measures, within the limits of avoiding mass unemployment, can be effective in dealing with a balance of payments deficit. Eliminations of excess demand must directly reduce imports and increase exports, and it may also have useful secondary effects through prices. To the extent that domestic prices are determined by aggregate demand, either through profit margins or indirectly through wages and other factor costs, they will fall as demand is decreased. This fall further reduces imports by encouraging substitution of local for imported goods in domestic expenditures, and it will also stimulate foreign demands for exports.

Governments may achieve these price effects more directly by using particular fiscal measures. Import prices, to domestic users, can be raised by tariffs, and such a rise has much the same effect as a fall in domestic prices caused by a reduction of aggregate demand. The import surcharge imposed by the British government for six months, in 1966-7, is a recent example of such manipulation to protect a weak balance of payments. Export prices, to foreign users, can similarly be lowered by special subsidies or tax-rebates to those industries which produce export goods. The General Agreement on Trade and Tariffs, however, makes either of these types of action embarrassingly difficult for manufactured goods, although anything seems to go in the case of primary exports.

What if fiscal or monetary measures have succeeded in pushing down aggregate demand to a level which is just consistent with a politically acceptable level of unemployment, but there is still a troublesome deficit in the current balance of external payments? The politicians, or the electorate, may be persuaded to raise their idea of a proper level of unemployment so that fiscal and monetary measures can be applied more rigorously still. Yet higher taxes, reductions in social services or other public expenditures and greater unemployment are bound to be so unpopular that such a policy has narrow limits of acceptability in a democracy. From the economist's standpoint, moreover, it is wasteful for resources to be idle, and some better solution of the problem has to be sought. The two alternatives most commonly advocated are import controls and devaluation.

16.2 Import Controls

At first sight, it may appear obvious that controls could improve the current balance to any desired extent simply by cutting back imports hard enough. We have, however, also to consider the demand pressures generated by such a cut, as these make for difficulties in enforcing controls and in maintaining exports. For import controls, to the extent that they succeed in their direct purpose, must add to those pressures which have already been great enough to cause the external deficit. Remembering our social accounting formulae we have

$$Y = C + G + I + X - M$$
$$\text{or } S = Y - (C + G) = I + B$$

so that

$$B = S - I.$$

An improvement in the current of payments, B, accordingly, adds to aggregate demand unless there is a corresponding rise in the propensity to save or a fall in the propensity to invest.

By themselves, import controls do nothing to bring about the required changes in the two propensities. Consumers will not save what can no longer be spent on excluded imports but will switch their expenditure to domestic substitutes. Producers will increase their investment demands in order to expand facilities for producing domestic substitutes. Aggregate demand, already excessive enough to cause an external deficit, must further increase as import controls reduce that deficit. Some of the additional pressure leads to additional demands for imports and so to greater incentives for evading the controls or corrupting those who administer them. And, even if the controls are fully efficient, governments are likely to sanction additional imports of materials and equipment for those producers who seek to provide substitutes for excluded imports. In countries which lack capital goods industries, and have moderate to high capital-output ratios for other industries, such demands for additional imports may well exceed in value the imports which are directly excluded by the controls. The saving in imports may thus become illusory.

The other awful possibility is that exports are reduced by the greater pressure of demand caused by import controls. This reduction may come about quickly if export goods can be readily diverted from foreign to domestic markets. If, however, they are specialized and narrow in range, the decline may be slow, and caused by a diversion of resources from export production to import substitution as aggregate demand raises both commodity and factor prices. Export industries would then have to raise their prices, lose foreign customers and curtail production; or, if export prices are fixed by world markets, export industries could not afford to produce so much as before owing to higher costs.

For these reasons import control cannot be really successful without some measure of deflation to damp down the extra pressure put on aggregate demand by import controls. But we are not fully back to the policy of correcting an external deficit by reducing aggregate demand because the required deflation is less with import controls than without them. This may be shown by the diagram opposite.[1]

The initial situation, without controls, is an equilibrium at E, where demands for imports and home produced goods are in balance at the point of tangency of an aggregate demand line, $Y_1 Y_1'$, to a community indifference curve,[2] I_3. But there is an external deficit, say FE. Straight out deflation could eliminate this deficit by reducing aggregate demand to $Y_3 Y_3'$; for at the new equilibrium, E', EF has been wiped out. But if controls directly wipe out the deficit then aggregate demand has to be

[1] M. F. W. Hemming and W. M. Corden, *Economic Journal*, 1958.
[2] These curves are explained by T. de Scitovsky, *Review of Economic Studies*, 1942.

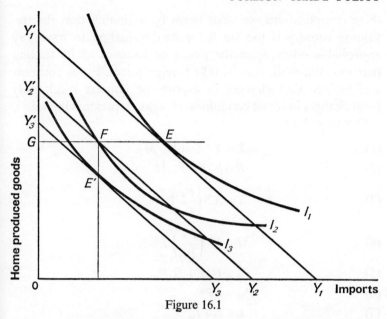

Figure 16.1

reduced only to $Y_2 Y_2'$. There is no longer equilibrium, as F is not a point of tangency between a community indifference curve and an aggregate demand line, but real income, and hence employment, is higher along the community indifference curve, I_2, than along I_3.

It is possible, therefore, for import controls to reduce the degree of deflation required for eliminating an external deficit. That is about all one can say for them. They are inadequate, by themselves, for that purpose, and always disappoint naive expectations unless accompanied by sufficient deflation. Nor can they be anything but a second-rate solution because, preventing the attainment of full economic equilibrium, they must involve a misallocation of productive resources which is harmful to long-term growth. But, as allocation is more a problem of micro-economics than of macro-economics, it will not be pursued here.

16.3 Devaluation in a Small Country
Devaluation is a simple measure but can have complicated repercussions upon the balance of payments. In order to reduce

189

these complications we shall begin by assuming that the devaluing country is too small for its devaluation to have any appreciable effect upon the prices or incomes of its trading partners. We shall, that is, take foreign prices, P_f, as constant and assume that changes in exports or imports result only from changes in home conditions. (L again represents liquidity).

Our model is:

$$(1) \qquad Y = Y^* + \mu(X - M)$$

$$(2) \qquad B = P_x X - P_m M$$

$$(3) \qquad X = X^* \left(\frac{P_x}{P_m}\right)^{-b}$$

$$(4) \qquad M = Y^\alpha \left(\frac{P_x}{P_m}\right)^\beta L^\gamma$$

$$(5) \qquad P_x = \Pi_1 Y + \Pi_2 P_m$$

$$(6) \qquad P_m = R P^*_f$$

$$(7) \qquad L = B + L_0$$

The first equation could be obtained from the income identity

$$Y = E + X - M$$

and from the expenditure function

$$E = E^* + eY$$

if we put

$$\mu = \frac{1}{1-e} \text{ and } Y^* = \mu E^*.$$

The second equation is an identity for the current balance of payments valued, as are other variables in the home currency. The third and fourth equations give the foreign demand for exports and the home demand for imports as depending upon the ratio of export to import prices, and the home demand for imports as depending further upon domestic income and domestic liquidity. The fifth equation gives export (supply) prices partly as demand-determined (Π_1) and partly as cost-determined (Π_2). Import prices are simply the constant foreign prices multiplied by the exchange rate, R, which is, itself, expressed as the price for a given amount of foreign currency in terms of the domestic currency. Liquidity necessarily increases by the value of a favourable external balance, or decreases by the value of an unfavourable external balance.

Measurement is such that all prices, quantities or values are initially taken, in index number form, as unity. It would then follow, noting that

$$dP_m = dR \text{ and } dL = dB$$

(8) $\qquad dY = \mu(dX - dM)$

(9) $\qquad dB = dX + dP_x - dM - dR$

(10) $\qquad dX = b(dR - dP_x)$

(11) $\qquad dM = \alpha dY - \beta(dP_x - dR) + \gamma dB$

(12) $\qquad dP_x = \Pi_1 dY + \Pi_2 dR$

These results can be put in the matrix form

(13)
$$
\begin{bmatrix}
1 & 0 & -\mu & \mu & 0 \\
0 & 1 & -1 & 1 & -1 \\
0 & 0 & 1 & 0 & b \\
-\alpha & -\gamma & 0 & 1 & -\beta \\
-\Pi_1 & 0 & 0 & 0 & 1
\end{bmatrix}
\begin{bmatrix}
\dfrac{dY}{dR} \\[2mm]
\dfrac{dB}{dR} \\[2mm]
\dfrac{dX}{dR} \\[2mm]
\dfrac{dM}{dR} \\[2mm]
\dfrac{dP_x}{dR}
\end{bmatrix}
=
\begin{bmatrix}
0 \\ -1 \\ b \\ -\beta \\ \Pi_2
\end{bmatrix}
$$

Solving then, by Cramer's rule, and using Δ for the determinant of the matrix of coefficients, we obtain

(14) $\qquad \dfrac{dB}{dR} = \left(\dfrac{1 - \Pi_2}{\Delta}\right)\left[(b+\beta-1) - \mu\alpha\right], \; \Delta > 0.$

This result may be interpreted in the following ways.

(a) If prices are wholly demand-determined, so that $\Pi_2 = 0$, and if domestic income is held constant, so that $\mu\alpha$ can be disregarded, then the condition for devaluation to improve the

191

current balance of payments is that the sum of the price-elasticities of demand for exports and imports exceeds unity.

(b) If domestic income increases as a result of the devaluation, then the above condition has to be strengthened to an extent depending upon the multiplier, μ, and the income-elasticity of demand for imports, α.

(c) The condition is further weakened to the extent that export prices are cost-determined and have an import content. In the extreme case that Π_2 becomes unity it is obvious from (14), that devaluation would have no effect upon the balance of payments but would merely raise prices and increase the burden of external debt.

The last two results point to the need to prevent domestic incomes or prices from responding to the higher export receipts or import prices which devaluation brings. Strong fiscal controls, that is, or strong measures to keep down incomes and prices are required if the full benefit of devaluation is to be obtained.

16.4 Devaluation with much Unemployment

The above model is, of course, not adequate if a country is big enough for its devaluation to affect other countries. Here the most useful simplification is to assume that both exports and imports are in perfectly elastic supply because of considerable unemployment both in the devaluing country and in other countries. As we shall see, this is the most favourable state of affairs for a successful devaluation by a large country.

Komiya[1] has put forward the following theoretical model in order to explain various contributions towards an analysis of this problem. He assumes that there are two countries, each producing only one good, X_1 and X_2^* respectively, which it exports to the other country and that both goods are in perfectly elastic supply at world prices which remain constant under devaluation. Variables for the foreign country are distinguishable by an asterisk.

[1] *The Economic Studies Quarterly*, December 1966. I regret that the mathematical argument has to be rather difficult.

We have, then, in our notation and with some rearrangement of his model:

(1)
$$Y = p_1 X_1 + A$$
$$Y^* = p_2^* X_2^* + A^*$$

(2)
$$X_1 = D_1 + D_1^*$$
$$X_2^* = D_2 + D_2^*$$

where the D's denote demands for the two goods. If now $L - L_0$ denotes change in *money* balances, we have

(3)
$$Y = p_1 D_1 + p_2 D_2 + L - L_0$$
$$Y^* = p_1^* D_1^* + p_2^* D_2^* + L^* - L_0^*$$

so that the current balance of payments is

(4)
$$B = (Y - p_1 D_1) - p_2 D_2 = L - L_0$$

Furthermore

(5)
$$p_1 = p_2^*$$
$$p_1 = p_1^* R$$
$$p_2 = p_2^* R$$

but initially all p and R are taken as unity. The demand functions are

(6)
$$D_i = D_i (p_1, p_2, Y, L_0) \qquad\qquad i = 1, 2$$
$$D_i^* = D_i^* (p_1^*, p_2^*, Y^*, L_0^*)$$

(7)
$$L = L (p_1, p_2, Y, L_0)$$
$$L^* = L^* (p_1^*, p_2^*, Y^*, L_0^*).$$

It follows from (4) and (7) that

(8)
$$\frac{dB}{dR} = \frac{\partial L}{\partial p_1}\frac{dp_1}{dR} + \frac{\partial L}{\partial p_2}\frac{dp_2}{dR} + \frac{\partial L}{\partial Y}\frac{dY}{dR}$$

and from (5) that, as the two goods are in perfectly elastic supply and devaluation affects only their import prices,

(9)
$$\frac{dp_1}{dR} = 0 = \frac{dp_2^*}{dR}$$

193

$$\frac{dp_2}{dR} = 1 = -\frac{dp_1^*}{dR}$$

It thus follows from (1) and (9) that

(10)
$$\frac{dY}{dR} = \frac{dX_1}{dR}$$
$$\frac{dY^*}{dR} = \frac{dX_2^*}{dR}.$$

Hence (8) becomes

(11)
$$\frac{dB}{dR} = \frac{\partial L}{\partial p_2} + h\frac{dX_1}{dR}$$

where $h = \dfrac{\partial L}{\partial Y}$ is the marginal propensity to hoard.

We have next to differentiate (2) with respect to R, obtaining

(12)
$$\frac{dX_1}{dR} = \frac{\partial D_1}{\partial p_2} + \frac{\partial D_1}{\partial Y}\frac{dX_1}{dR} - \frac{\partial D_1^*}{\partial p_1^*} + \frac{\partial D_1^*}{\partial y^*}\frac{dX_2^*}{dR}$$

Denoting the marginal propensities to spend on each good as

$$m_i = \frac{\partial D_i}{\partial Y} \text{ and } m_i^* = \frac{\partial D_i^*}{\partial Y^*} \qquad i = 1, \ 2$$

we rewrite (12), and obtain a similar expression for $\dfrac{dX_2^*}{dR}$;

(13)
$$(1 - m_1)\frac{dX_1}{dR} - m_1^*\frac{dX_2^*}{dR} = \frac{\partial D_1}{\partial p_2} - \frac{\partial D_1^*}{\partial p_1^*}$$
$$-m_2\frac{dX_1}{dR} + (1 - m_2^*)\frac{dX_2^*}{dR} = \frac{\partial D_2}{\partial p_2} - \frac{\partial D_2^*}{\partial p_1^*}.$$

Noting from partial differentiation of (3) with respect to Y that

(14)
$$1 = h + m_1 + m_2 = h^* + m_1^* + m_2^*$$

194

FOREIGN TRADE POLICY

we may combine (11) and (13) in the matrix equation

(15)
$$
\begin{bmatrix}
1 & -h & 0 \\
0 & (1-m_1) & -m_1^* \\
0 & -m_2 & (1-m_2^*)
\end{bmatrix}
\begin{bmatrix}
\dfrac{dB}{dR} \\[2mm]
\dfrac{dX_1}{dR} \\[2mm]
\dfrac{dX_2^*}{dR}
\end{bmatrix}
=
\begin{bmatrix}
\dfrac{\partial L}{\partial p_2} \\[2mm]
\dfrac{\partial D_1}{\partial p_2} - \dfrac{\partial D_1^*}{\partial p_1^*} \\[2mm]
\dfrac{\partial D_2}{\partial p_2} - \dfrac{\partial D_2^*}{\partial p_1^*}
\end{bmatrix}
$$

At this point we go back to (3) in order to differentiate it partially with respect to p_2, again remembering that outputs are perfectly elastic;

$$0 = p_1 \frac{\partial D_1}{\partial p_2} + D_2 + p_2 \frac{\partial D_2}{\partial p_2} + \frac{\partial L}{\partial p_2}$$

or

$$\frac{\partial D_1}{\partial p_2} = -D_2(1-\eta) - \frac{\partial L}{\partial p_2}$$

$$\eta = -\frac{p_2 \partial D_2}{D_2 \partial p_2}.$$

Similarly we obtain, by differentiating with respect to p_1^*,

$$\frac{\partial D_2^*}{\partial p_1^*} = -D_1^*(1-\eta^*) - \frac{\partial L^*}{\partial p_1^*}$$

$$\eta^* = -\frac{p_1^* \partial D_1^*}{D_1^* \partial p_1^*}.$$

If, then, the current balance was initially zero so that

$$p_2 D_2 = p_1^* D_1^* = D_2 = D_1^*$$

we could rewrite (15) as

(16)
$$
\begin{bmatrix}
1 & -h & 0 \\
0 & (1-m_1) & -m_1^* \\
0 & -m_2 & (1-m_2^*)
\end{bmatrix}
\begin{bmatrix}
\dfrac{dB}{dR} \\[2mm]
\dfrac{dX_1}{dR} \\[2mm]
\dfrac{dX_2^*}{dR}
\end{bmatrix}
=
\begin{bmatrix}
\dfrac{\partial L}{\partial p_2} \\[2mm]
D_2(\eta + \eta^* - 1) - \dfrac{\partial L}{\partial p_2} \\[2mm]
-D_2(\eta + \eta^* - 1) + \dfrac{\partial L^*}{\partial p_1^*}
\end{bmatrix}
$$

The solution for $\dfrac{dB}{dR}$ could then be found as

(17) $$\frac{dB}{dR} = \frac{hh^*}{\Delta}\left[D_2\left(\eta+\eta^*-1\right)+\left(\frac{m^*_1}{h^*}\right)\frac{\partial L^*}{\partial p_1^*}+\frac{m_2}{h}\frac{\partial L}{\partial p_2}\right]$$

where Δ is now the determinant of the coefficient matrix in (16); η is the price-elasticity of domestic demand for imports of η^* the price-elasticity of foreign demand for exports.

Our conclusions here are:

(a) If liquidity effects are ignored, the current balance of payments is improved by devaluation provided, again, that the sum of the price-elasticities of demand for imports and exports is greater than unity.[1]

(b) If, as Harberger[2] has assumed, demand for money balances depends only upon real income, and so decreases as prices of goods increase, then a stronger condition is needed. For, as may be verified, we would then have

$$\frac{\partial L^*}{\partial p_1^*} = -h^*D_2, \quad \frac{\partial L}{\partial p_2} = -hD_2$$

and the condition for successful devaluation would be

$$\eta+\eta^*>1+m_1+m_2^*;$$

i.e. the sum of the price-elasticities for imports in the two countries would have to exceed unity plus the sum of their marginal propensities to import.

(c) On the other hand, a weaker condition will hold if, as Hahn[3] has assumed, money balances are a gross substitute for goods so that demand for money balances increases as the prices of goods increase. For in this case both $\dfrac{\partial L^*}{\partial p_1^*}$ and $\dfrac{\partial L}{\partial p_2}$ would be positive.

[1] This condition always holds if there are only two goods in consumers' budgets; cp. Komiya, op. cit., p. 20.

[2] A. C. Harberger, *Journal of Political Economy*, 1950.

[3] F. H. Hahn, *Review of Economic Studies*, 1959.

16.5 Devaluation with little Unemployment

The above results crucially depend upon the assumption of perfectly elastic supply for each country's exports (or imports). Such full employment, at home and abroad, as made export supplies quite unresponsive to the price changes which follow devaluation would throw everything upon the assumption made about demand for liquidity. For we would have, as before,

$$\frac{dB}{dR} = \frac{dL}{dR}$$

but L would now depend only upon prices as outputs would be rigid.

On Hahn's assumption that liquid balances are a gross substitute for goods, higher prices in the devaluing country would increase its demand for liquidity and so improve its current balance of payments through an associated decrease in demands for goods at home. At the same time, the improvement would be strengthened by a corresponding increase in demands for its exports abroad. But on Harberger's assumption that demand for money holdings depends only upon real income, which could now only decline through the price increases caused by devaluation, the current balance of payments would worsen.

There are, accordingly, theoretical doubts regarding the outcome of devaluation under conditions approximating those of full employment. Even if Harberger's assumption is not fully acceptable (it involves an element of 'money illusion'), most economists recognize that the gain of liquidity from an immediately successful devaluation poses a real danger to any permanent improvement in the current balance. Johnson,[1] for example sums up a complex discussion of this problem by saying that unless devaluation is accompanied by deflationary measures to hold down aggregate spending it causes an inflationary excess of aggregate demand over aggregate supply, leading to price increases which counteract the direct effect of

H. G. Johnson, *International Trade and Economic Growth*, (1958), pp. 166–7

devaluation in switching domestic spending from exports and imports to other goods. Alexander[1] has shown that such inflation may, under some conditions, curtail real spending; but Johnson regards the possibility as so dubious that it helps to explain 'both the prevalence of scepticism about, and hostility towards, exchange rate adjustment as a means of curing balance-of-payments disquilibria and the fact that historical experience can be adduced in support of the proposition that devaluation is a doubtful remedy'.

Harrod[2] has expressed a stronger scepticism.

The case against devaluing, when there is internal inflationary pressure and external deficit, is that, even if devaluation has a remedial effect on the external balance, it will increase the internal inflationary pressure. . . . It is a dangerous remedy when there is internal inflationary pressure, as in Britain in 1949. It has the effect of increasing demand-pull inflation. . . . There is another aspect no less important. . . . It has a direct effect on cost-push inflation. . . . A strong rise in import prices is bound to have an important effect upon the cost of living. It will also have an indirect effect by provoking (and justifying) wage demands.

(Recall here the analysis of 16.4.)

Historical experience of the 1949 deaaluations, at least, seems to bear out the inflationary effects of devaluation and so the rather fleeting nature of any benefits which it may confer under conditions of full employment. When Britain devalued then its example was widely followed, and J. S. Pollak[1] studied the comparative effects of this widespread devaluation with reference to the six devaluing countries and three non-devaluing countries, all in Western Europe. He reached these conclusions for the period 1949–50:

Apparently the devaluations increased the volume of exports to the United States by an amount little more than enough to offset the fall of about 15 per cent in dollar export prices. It may be further

[1] S. Alexander, *I.M.F. Staff Papers*, 1952.
[2] R .F. Harrod, *Policy Against Inflation*, (1958), pp. 134–5.
[3] *I.M.F. Staff Papers*, 1951–52.

estimated that the devaluations were responsible for a 10 per cent increase in the dollar value of Western Europe's exports to other markets on the Western Hemisphere, Canada and Latin America. With imports generally controlled, the effects of the devaluations appeared much more in the reduction of pressure on the control authorities than in the statistics.

But Pollak was spreaking of the impact effect of devaluation which would weaken as devaluation contributed to demand pressures. In this connection the Stockholm Konjunkturinstitut found that, by 1952, the immediate fall in relative prices had been greatly reduced if not entirely wiped out. It compared prices and labour costs in Belgium, Britain, France, Germany, Italy, Sweden, Switzerland and the United States.

By the beginning of 1952, the immediate effect of the devaluation on wholesale prices, calculated in terms of dollars, had been practically eliminated. Six of the eight countries showed index figures between 103 and 108 (1948 = 100), only two of the countries differing appreciably from the rest; France by having a sharper price increase and Italy by having a smaller.

This evidence, accordingly, shows that the immediate effect of the 1949 devaluations was weak, and that any benefits which they conferred were soon lost through inflation in the devaluing countries, although that inflation owed much to other causes than the devaluations themselves.

Britain's further devaluation in 1967 appeared to have, in some respects, a better chance of success. It was much less widely followed by other countries and could therefore have a greater impact upon the British balance of payments. It could also have had a more durable effect in that the authorities used stern fiscal measures in order to prevent domestic prices from so rising as to wipe out the competitive advantage from devaluation to industries which can produce exports or substitutes for imports. A further attempt, too, was made in this direction by an extension of the policy for holding down wages and other incomes. The task, nevertheless, is a difficult one because of the magnitude of the correction needed in the British account, the strength of inflationary forces, the weakness of income policy, depression of some export markets and the widespread speculation against leading currencies in favour of gold. Good luck, as well as good management, would be needed for success, and there was little sign of success in the first eight months after the devaluation. But whatever the outcome, macro-economists, at least, are gaining a further insight into the working of devaluation in an important country at a high level of employment.

Index

Accelerator
  in multiplier-accelerator
  models, 26, 32, 36
  and capital-output ratio, 60
  in long-run, 65
acceleration principle
  and inventory cycles, 61–2
  lagged, 65–6
  see also multiplier-accelerator
  models
Ackley, G.
  built-in stabilizers, 156–7
ad hoc policy,. 145
aggregating equations, 18–19, 21
aggregate demand, 16, 99, 127–8,
  149
  and prices, 157–8
  and wages, 173, 184
  and external balance, 185–8
aggregate investment, 17
aggregate saving, 17
aggregate supply, 82, 99, 127–8,
  133, 142
Alexander, S.
  devaluation, 197
Arrow, K.
  production function, 84
Australia, 100
autonomous influence, 21

Balance of external payments, 185
  see also devaluation
balanced budget theorem, 148–9

Bank of England, 161
  banks see central and commercial banks
basic material imports, 79
Bassie, K. L.
  import demand, 77
behaviour relations, 23
Bergstrom, A. R.
  model for New Zealand, xii,
  93–5
bonds, 70–1, 135
Bronfenbrenner, M.
  effects of distribution of
  income, 53–4
  testing of liquidity function,
  72–3
Brown, A. J.
  demand function for liquidity,
  72
Brown, M.
  demand for labour, 87
Brown, T. M.
  consumption function, 50, 52
  liquidity, 54
Brownlie, A. D.
  model for New Zealand, 93–5
Brumberg, R.
  consumption function, 51
budget surplus, 148–9
built-in stabilizers, 154–5, 157
business, 5, 9
  forecasting of output, 90–3
buying sector, 105

capacity principle, 64–5, 67
   in Dutch model, 91
   in New Zealand model, 94
Capital
   as single aggregate, 99
   and productive sectors, 100
capital consumption allowances,
   see depreciation
capital formation, 6, 9, 11, 15, 99
   see also investment
capital gains, 14, 49, 54
capital market, 70–1, 164–5
capital-output model, 32–5
   and capacity principle, 63–5
capital-output ratio, *see* accelerator
cash, 69
C.B.I., 181
central banks
   control of non-bank lenders,
   166
   purchases of bonds, 135–6,
   161–2, 163–4
   rate of interest, 159, 161
   supply of money and liquidity,
   162–5
Chenery, H. B.
   capacity principle, 64
   production function, 84
   treatment of imports as inputs,
   105
cheque deposits, 69
Clark, G. C.
   consumption function, 49
   production account, 100
Clark, P. G.
   treatment of imports as inputs,
   105
Cobb-Douglas production fun-
tion, 64, 84
commercial banks, 75–6, 159, 163,
166
   see also financial intermediaries
Commission on Money and Credit,
56, 167

consumer durables, 8, 56, 70
consumption
   determinants of, 49–58
   in national income account,
   5, 16–17
   in interindustry account, 100
   classical theory of, 125–30, 168
consumption functions
   and disposable real income, 49
   and previous consumption, 50,
   52, 55, 56, 58
   and changes in income distribution, 52–4
   and expected or permanent
   income, 51–2, 57
   and interest and liquidity, 54–5
   and previous income, 50, 55–6,
   58
   and liquid assets, 54–5, 56, 58
Corden, M.
   import controls, 188
cost-determined prices, 117, 120,
131, 158, 176, 192
cost-push inflation, 170–2, 175
Council of Economic Advisers, 182
Council on Prices, Productivity,
   and Incomes, 180
Cramer's rule, 191
'creeping inflation', 171–2
Croft-Murray, G.
   treatment of competitive imports, 105
Culbertson, J.
   movement of interest rates, 161
cycles
   in income, 30–2, 35
   irregularity of, 35
   in inventories, 60–3
   in fixed investment, 34–5

Darling, P. G.
   inventory cycles, 62
decision model, 146

definitional relation, 16–17, 22
in Leontief's model, 112
deflation
and external balance, 186, 192, 197, 199
and import controls, 188–9
De Leeuw, F.
theory of fixed investment, 66–7
demand
for imports, 77, 79
for inputs, 103, 114–15, 120
for labour, 82–7
for liquidity, 129, 133–4
see also aggregate demand, consumption functions, excess demand, investment
demand-pull inflation, 173–4
depreciation or capital consumption, 9, 11, 100, 102
funds, 65
devaluation, 146, 176
of sterling, 185, 196, 197
in a small country, 189–92
with unemployed resources, 192–6
with little unemployment, 196–9
and excess demand, 197
Dicks-Mireaux, L. A.
and wage changes, 174
direct taxes, rates of, 22–3, 147–8
discount rate or bank rate, 159, 161, 163
see also interest, rate of
dollar area, U.K. exports to, 81
domestic expenditure function, 93
Dow, J. C. R.
wage determination, 174
Duesenberry, J. S.
capacity principle, 65
relative income hypotheses, 52, 57
saving-income ratios, 50–1
dummy sales, 7, 8

Durbin-Watson statistics, 43

E.C.E. countries, 183
Eckstein, O.
appreciation of De Leeuw's hypotheses, 66–7
profits and wage rates, 175
relative income hypotheses, 57
economic growth, see growth model
econometric tests, 40–5
Eisner, R.
inventory investment, 62
lagged acceleration principle, 65–6
elasticity of substitution, 83
in Cobb-Douglas function, 84
in homohypallagic function, 85
employment, see demand for labour
also full employment
equations, types of, 22
equilibrium of economy, 130, 134, 137, 139–40, 142–3
excess demand, 130, 172, 186, 197
exchange control, 146
exchange rates, 185
see also devaluation
'expectational' variable, 67
exponential relations, 19
exports
demand for, 79–81, 185–6
in Dutch model, 91
in national accounts, 15–16, 100, 109
and import controls, 188
external sector, 4, 6, 15
valuation of transactions, 105

Factor incomes, 6, 100
Federal Reserve Board
and monetary policy, 159, 160, 161, 163, 166

final demands
contributions of sectors, 100, 103
derivation of intermediate demands from, 82, 114–15
effect of changes in, 115–18
final outputs, 6, 99
and imports, 77
financial intermediaries, 76, 159
and liquidity structure, 163
and business investment, 165
control of, 166
fiscal policy, 69, 146–58
instruments of, 147–8
compensatory action, 152–3
and demand inflation, 157–8
and balance of payments deficit, 185
Fisher, A. G. B.
classification of industries, 100
Fisher, I. L.
real balance effect, 138
food imports in U.K., 79
forecasting models
United States, 88–9
New Zealand, 93–4
short-term accuracy of, 95
foreign exchange, 3, 186
see also devaluation
Friedman, M.
permanent income hypothesis, 51–2, 72
automatic monetary policy, 155–6
Fromm, G.,
relative income hypothesis, 57
full employment
and reduction in wage rate, 168–9
and stability of money wages, 158, 172–6
as objective, 3, 145
functional finance, 151–3

General Agreement on Tariffs and Trade, 186
gold and dollar reserves of U.K., 78–9
Goldberger, A. S.
demand for imports, 78
demand for liquidity, 72
estimates of marginal propensity to consume, 53
investment and capacity, 64
production function, 86
wages and degree of unemployment, 137
wages and prices, 175
Goodwin, R. C.
lop-sided accelerator models, 36
Government consumption, 5, 7, 16, 99, 100, 115–16, 147–8, 154
Government capital formation, 13, 147–50, 154, 155
Government debt management, 160
Government factor income, 16
Government income and expenditure account, 4, 100
Government saving, 5, 15, 17
Government objectives, 145
Griliches, Z.
consumption function, 56
growth models, 3, 26, 27–8, 29, 35, 36
Gurley, J. G.
central bank controls, 166
financial intermediaries, 76

Hahn, F.
devaluation, 196, 197
Hansen, A. H.
managed compensatory fiscal program, 152
Hansen, B.
fiscal instruments, 148
Harberger, A. C.
devaluation, 196, 197

Harrod, R. F.
  devaluation, 197–8
Harrod-Domar model, 27–8
Hatanaka, M.
  results of input-control analysis, 121
Hawtrey, R. G.
  interest rate policy, 162
Hemming, M. F. W.
  import controls, 188
Hicks, J. R.
  effect of income on investment, 59
    Keynesian model, 132–6
    lagged multiplier-accelerator model, 32
    lop-sided accelerator model, 36
Hines, A. G.
  model for wage changes, 174–5
homogeneity of sector outputs, 104
homohypallagic function, 84

Identities, 15–17, 22
imports
  and aggregate demand, 185
  and estimate of requirements for, 114–15
  and inventories, 77, 78
  and productive sectors, 100–3
  and tariffs, 186
  classification of, 105
  competitive and complementary, 105
  controls, 78–9, 187–9
  forecasting effects of changes in, 118–19
  forecasting of, in Netherlands, 91
  in New Zealand, 95
  see also demand, prices
import surcharge in U.K., 186
imputations, 8–9, 11–12

income
  aggregation of, 19–20
  disposable private, 16, 147, 154
  distribution of, 49, 52–3, 58, 141–3
  expected permanent, 51–2
  factor, 6, 16, 100
  government, 4, 12–13, 100
  policy, 176–84
  private, 4, 16
  relative income, 50–2
  see also interest, profits, wages
indirect taxes, 22–3, 102, 147–8, 176–7
industrial classification, 104
inflation, 3
  avoidance of, 125
  control of, 157–8
  causes of, 170–6
  and devaluation, 197–8
  and wages policy, 176–84
interest in national accounts, 13–14
interest, rate of
  effect on consumption, 49, 54–7
  effect on investment, 59, 66, 67–8, 162, 167
    natural or normal, 131
    structure of, 161, 164, 165–6
    and Keynesian model, 69–71, 132–5, 136, 140
    and liquidity, 70–5, 164
    and Riccardo-Wicksell model, 128, 143
  see also discount rate
intermediate goods, 6, 99, 102–3
internal financing or liquidity, 65, 66, 165
International Monetary Fund, 185
inventories or stocks, 5, 6
  influence of interest on, 162
  cyclical movement of, 36, 60–3
  and imports, 77, 78
  valuation of changes in, 9–10

205

investment
    aggregate, 14, 15, 17
    determinants of, 59–60, 162, 163, 165, 167
    in 'Classical' theory, 128–9
    in fixed capital, 63–8, 89, 90–1
    in stocks, 60–2
    see also accelerator, capital formation, depreciation

Japan
    imports in, 78
    investments in, 67–8
    transaction matrix, 104
Johnson, H. G.
    devaluation, 197

Kaldor, N.
    and full employment equilibrium, 141–3
Keynes, J. M. (Lord)
    consumption function, 49
    cost-determined prices, 169
    criticism of 'classical' theory, 131–2, 134, 169
    effect of interest on consumption, 54, 162
    effect of interest on investment, 59, 162
    motives for holding liquid balances, 70–1
    public spending, 140–50
    liquidity trap, 71, 134–5
Klein, L.
    consumption functions, 50, 52, 55
    effect of interest on consumption, 54
    effect of liquidity on consumption, 55
    export functions, 80–1
    import functions, 78–9
    investment functions, 64

    marginal propensity to consume, 53
    on 'liquidity trap', 72
    production functions, 86–7
    Keynesian model, 136–7, 140, 157
    wage-adjustment, 175
Komiya, R.
    devaluation model, 192–6
Konjunkturinstitut (Stockholm)
    on 1949 devaluations, 199
Kuh, E.
    fixed investment study, 65
Kuznets, S.
    saving-income ratios, 50–1

Labour
    demand for, 82–6, 100, 114
    market, 126, 131, 139, 168–70
    supply of, 87
lags
    effect on corrective measures, 153
    effect on forecasts, 89
    in capital-output model, 33, 36
    in consumption function, 49–50
    in multiplier-accelerator model 28, 32, 65
    in multiplier model, 24–5
    in investment function, 60, 66–7, 89
    'least squares' regression, 42, 43, 44
Lee, C. H.
    income distribution and consumption, 53–4
Leontief model, 110–14
    and changes in final demands, 115–16
    assumptions of, 111, 117
    demand for primary inputs, 114–15
    limitations of, 120–1
    price analysis, 117–19

Leontief model—*continued*
  uses of, 119–20
  working of, 112–13
Lerner, A. P.
  functional finance, 151
Levenbach, M. G.
  wages policy, 179–80
liquidity, 69, 163
  and consumption, 54–8, 138–41
  and investment, 64–5, 138–41, 160, 162–7
  and budget surplus, 149
  and external balance, 191, 196
  demand for, 70–6, 133–6, 137, 196, 197
  'trap', 71–2, 136, 141
loans, supply of, 160, 163
Lucas, R.
  consumption function, 56
Lundberg, E.
  inventory cycles, 61

Macro-economic relations, 18–23
  testing of, 40–1
Maddala, G. S.
  consumption function, 56
marginal products derived from production functions, 83, 84
marginal propensity to consume, 27
  and income distribution, 52–3
  long-run, 56–7, 141–2
marginal propensity to invest, 59–60
marginal propensity to save, 27
marginal propensity to spend, 23
marginal rate of substitution, 83, 84, 85
Marshall, A.
  real balance effect, 138
matrix
  generalized, 109
  of social accounts, 5

technology, 111
Mayer, T.
  testing of liquidity functions, 72–3
Meade, J.
  money supply, 75
Meltzer, A. H.
  wealth and liquidity, 73
Metzler, L. A.
  and inventory cycles, 61
Meyer, J. R.
  determinants of fixed investment, 65
micro-economic theory, 18–21
Minhas, B.
  production function, 84
models, 22–3
  see also growth models, forecasting models
Modigliani, F.
  consumption function, 51
  supply of money, 75
monetary policy
  automatic, 155
  instruments of, 159–60
  limitations of, 165–7
  scope of, 69
  and full employment, 134–5, 141
  and liquidity, 161–5
  and rate of interest, 160–1
money, 69
  as store of value, 70, 74
  supply, 73, 75
money market
  and 'classical theory', 129
  and equilibrium of interest and income, 133–4, 136
multiple correlation coefficient, 42
multiplier, 23–4, 59
  effect of income distribution on, 53
multiplier-accelerator models
  unlagged, 26–7

multiplier-accelerator models—
continued
lagged, 28–9

National Board for Prices and Incomes, 181
national capital account, 4, 5, 6, 15, 99, 100
national expenditure, 16, 99
national income account, 3–4, 5, 16
National Incomes Commission, 180–1
national budget policy, 145–6
national production account, 4, 6–7
breakdown of, 99–102
advantages of breakdown, 103
problems of measurement, 8–9
Netherlands
price controls in, 183
wages policy in, 176–80
Netherlands Central Planning Bureau
estimates of marginal propensity to consume, 53
export demand function, 80
import demand function, 77–8
investment function, 65
planning model, 90–3
production function, 86–7
use of input-output analysis, 120–1
New Zealand
forecasting model, 93–4
productive sectors, 100
transaction matrix, 104, 107
normal distribution, 40
Norway
planning in price controls in, 183

O.E.C.D.
reports on prices, 182
Ohlin, B.
deficit finance, 150
oligopolist pricing, 172, 183

open-market operations, 159, 161–3
output, *see* aggregate supply

Partial elasticities of demand, 19, 73–4, 192, 195, 196
Patinkin, D.
interest and aggregate demand, 140, 162
liquidity and aggregate demand, 54, 162
monetary policy, 135–6
'real balance effect', 138–40, 143
perfect competition and demands for factors, 64, 82–6
Phillips, A. W.
lags in corrective measures, 153
money wages and employment, 158, 173
Pigou, A. C.
real balance effect, 54, 138
planning, 90–3, 145–7
Pollak, J. S.
devaluation of 1949, 198–9
precautionary motive for liquidity, 70
prices
cost-determined, 117, 120, 131, 158, 192
demand-determined, 129–30, 140–1, 158–9, 170–6, 184
index of, 20, 99
stability and wage regulation, 145, 158, 176–84
and exports, 80–1
and imports, 77–9
in Leontief model, 117–19
price elasticities for imports and exports, 192, 196
production decision equation, 93
productive sectors, 99–100
interconnections of, 101–3
requirements of classification, 103–4

productivity and wage levels, 180–2
production
see also aggregate supply, 4–5
production functions, 82–7, 111, 127
profits, 6, 8, 9, 14
and investments, 33, 60, 65, 141–2
and saving, 49–50
and price increases, 172, 175
control of and income policy, 183
forecasting of, 91
profit maximisation
and demand for labour, 126
and investment, 64
and output, 82
property income, 6, 8
public works, see fiscal policy

Quantity theory of money, 130, 140

Radcliffe Report, 161–2, 163
'ratchet effect', 51
rate of interest and monetary policy, 130, 143
'real balance effect', 138–41, 143
real productive flows, 9, 99–101
regression analysis, 40–4
relative influences of variables, 44–5
relative income hypothesis, 50–1, 57
reserve requirements of Central Banks, 160
residual errors, 41–4
Ricardo, D., 125
Roberts, A. C.
on Dutch wage policy, 179–80
Robertson, D. H.
on Keynes, 136
Rosa, R. V.
monetary influences, 163, 166

Sales
in production account, 6, 99–101

Samuelson, P. A.
lagged multiplier-accelerator model, 32
Sargan, J. D.
devaluation, 176
wages and prices, 175–6
saving
effect of wealth upon, 55
in classical theory, 128–9
ratios to income, 50–1
see also marginal propensity to save, 128–9
savings deposit, 69, 74
Sayers, R. S.
monetary policy, 166
secondary industry, 100
sectors and sector accounts, 4, 5, 18, 99–101, 103, 105, 106, 108
securities, 70
serial correlation, 40, 43–4
Shaw, E. S.
financial intermediaries, 76
central bank control, 166
'significance' level, 43
Smith, W. G.
inventory fluctuations, 62
Smithies, A.
capacity principle, 65
fiscal policy, 152
social accounts, 3–15, 99, 107–8
Solow, R. M.
production function, 84
speculative motive for liquidity, 70–2
Sterling Area, 81
stocks, see inventories
Stone, R.
consumption function, 49
treatment of competitive, 105
generalized transactions matrix, 107–8
'stop-go' measures, 185
Strotz, R. H.
inventory investment, 62, 66

subsidy payments, rates of, 7, 16,
147–8
Suits, D. B.
consumption function, 56
supply, *see* aggregate supply
supply curve for labour, 126, 131,
139

Ta-Chung, Liu
forecasting model, 88–90
tariffs, 186
taxes and control of aggregate
demand, 154–6
see also direct and indirect
taxes
'technical coefficients', of production, 111
technical relations, 22, 88
technology matrix, 111–13
Teigen, R. L.
monetary model, 73–5
tertiary industry, 100–2
testing of theories, 40–4
Thornton, H.
monetary policy, 161
time deposits, 69
Tinbergen, J.
consumption function, 49, 52–3
effect of rate of interest, 162
investment function, 59–60
level of stocks, 60
test of acceleration principle,
63
wages policy, 196–7
Tintner, G. G.
supply function for labour, 87
Tobin, J.
liquidity function, 72
Tooke, T.
effect of interest rates, 162
transactions
in interindustry accounts, 99–
102, 104–5

in social accounts, 4–5
of government, 12–13
transaction matrices, 100, 106,
108, 109
transactions motive for liquidity, 70
transfers, 6–7, 13, 16
rates of payments for, 147–8,
155
transport sector, 105
T.U.C., 181

United Kingdom
balance of payments deficits,
185
devaluations, 185, 198, 199
export functions, 80–1
fiscal policy in, 152
import functions, 78–9
income policy in, 180–1
social accounting in, 3, 11, 12
transaction matrix for, 106–8
United Nations Organization
full employment measures, 151
social accounting, 3–4, 11, 12,
14
underdeveloped countries, 9
unemployment
avoidance of, 3, 125, 145
benefits, 154
fiscal policy, 138
involuntary, 131
monetary policy, 134–6
and inflation, 171
and wage rates, 173–6
see also labour
unions
in Netherlands, 177–8
in United Kingdom, 181
and cost inflation, 172, 175–6
United States
balance of payments, 185
financial intermediaries, 166
forecasting model, 88–90
incomes policy, 182

United States—*continued*
  social accounting, 3, 12
  transaction matrix, 104
  see also Federal Reserve Board

Wages
  in interindustry accounts, 100–2
  in social accounts, 6, 7, 8, 9, 13
wage-adjustment equations, 87, 172–6
wage rates
  and demand for labour, 83–7
  control of, 84, 146, 176
  effect of costs in, 132, 168–70
  in Dutch model, 91
  in Leontief model, 118–19
  see also labour
Wallace, N.
  consumption function, 56

Walras, L.
  general equilibrium, 110
wealth
  effect on liquidity, 72–3
  effect on saving or consumption, 54, 55, 58
weighted averages, 20, 21, 52
Wicksell, K.
  monetary theory, 125, 130–1, 138
Wilson, T. A.
  profits and unemployed, 175

Yamane, T.
  effect of income distribution in consumption, 53

Zellner, A.
  consumption function, 55–6